Healing from Trauma for Men

THE COURAGE METHOD

A Simple and Proven Way to Overcome Depression without Medication

Dylan Martinsen

Nighthawk
PUBLISHING CO.

ISBN:979-8-9912339-0-3

Copyright @ 2024. Dylan Martinsen. All rights reserved. No part of this book may be reproduced by any mechanical, photographic, or electronic process, or in the form of a phonographic recording; nor may it be stored in a retrieval system, transmitted, or otherwise be copied for public or private use—other than for "fair use" as brief quotations embodied in articles and reviews—without prior written permission of the publisher.

This publication is designed to provide accurate and authoritative information regarding the subject matter covered. It is sold with the understanding that the publisher is not engaged in rendering legal, accounting, or other professional services. If you require professional advice or other expert assistance, you should seek the services of a professional.

If you or someone you know is experiencing suicidal thoughts or a crisis, please reach out immediately to the Suicide Prevention Lifeline at 800-273-8255 or text HOME to the Crisis Text Line at 741741. These services are free and confidential.

Disclaimer: The author makes no guarantees to the results you'll achieve by reading this book. The journey requires risk and hard work. The results presented in this book represent results the author achieved over several years of continued effort. Your results may vary when undertaking this journey.

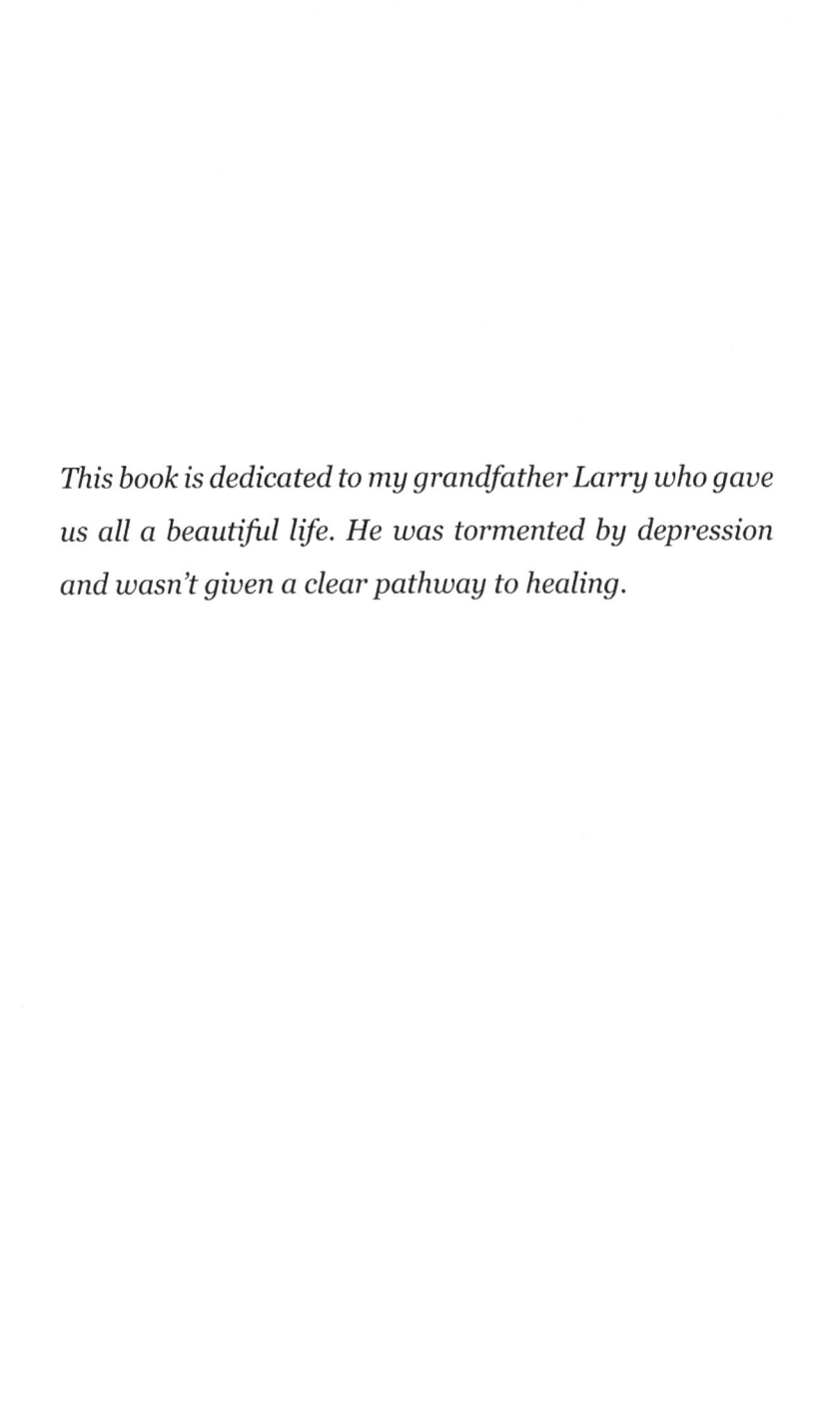

This book is dedicated to my grandfather Larry who gave us all a beautiful life. He was tormented by depression and wasn't given a clear pathway to healing.

"The answer to everything you want is found in the dark places you don't want to go."

—Dylan Martinsen

Contents

Introduction: Why This Book Exists 9

Part I: Understanding the Journey 21

    Chapter 1: Life after Depression 23

    Chapter 2: The Path of the Warrior 31

    Chapter 3: The 5 Hard and Ugly Truths about Overcoming Depression 43

    Chapter 4: The Secret Key to Overcoming Depression 67

    Chapter 5: The Catch 81

Part II: The Courage Method 87

    Chapter 6: The Warrior's Way 89

    Chapter 7.1: The 3 Arts of Self-Mastery 99

The Art of War 103

    Chapter 7.2: Understanding Depression 105

    Chapte 7.3: Compassionate Introspection 123

Chapter 7.4: The Depression Trap 133

Chapter 7.5: Fighting Depression 161

The Art of Alchemy 187

Chapter 7.6: Healing Your Pain 189

The Art of Help 205

Chapter 7.7: Gathering Your Party 207

Chapter 7.8: Audentis Fortuna Iuvat 225

Part III: The Journey Begins 229

Chapter 8: Releasing from Blame 231

Chapter 9: The 4-Phase Battle Plan 235

Chapter 10: Clear the Slate 245

Chapter 11: How to Find a Therapist in 30 days 251

Chapter 12: Conclusion 259

Resources 263

About the Author 271

INTRODUCTION:
Why This Book Exists

"Imagine a tree growing high on a mountaintop. If this tree grows too fast without first properly rooting itself, it becomes susceptible to being torn up and destroyed by the wind. If, however, it establishes a proper foundation and is content to grow gradually, it will enjoy a long life and a lofty view."

-Brian Browne Walker

I know your journey with depression has been long and taxing. There is an end in sight, and this book is going to help you get there. Before we get started, I just want to say I'm sorry for what you're going through. Whatever brought you here, you didn't deserve it, but you do deserve a clear pathway out. A pathway not only to feeling better but to complete transformation.

My goal is to change your mind about how you view your depression. I believe that the way we approach depression prevents us from overcoming depression. We attempt to push the horrible feelings away and suppress the feeling to get back to feeling good instead of investigating the heart of the problem.

Depression is a signal that something in your past is unresolved and needs not only your attention but your love. Take a moment with that. Did you notice something? Did your ears start to perk up with curiosity? Can you start to ask the questions, "What caused my depression? How do I resolve it? What are the tools and techniques to undo it?" With this questioning, you can see that introspection, learning new knowledge, and training new skills is required, and with that, your very own hero's journey emerges. You are not just pushing away all the bad feelings. You are being called to a journey that will transform your entire life experience.

That is what I want for you.

I wrote this book because we're in the midst of a silent men's mental health epidemic. In the last decade alone, rates of depression and suicide amongst men have skyrocketed. Contrary to what many would have you believe, the men who are being affected aren't at fault.

Why?

One Simple Reason:

The social standards for 'being a man' inhibit us from developing the skills needed to process trauma, leaving us depressed, anxious, confused, and living without vibrant purpose.

See, the example that has been set for us growing up does not give us the skills we need to live healthy and fulfilled lives. Instead, it teaches us to suppress our feelings, leaving us barely capable of processing life events and trauma. Not only does it cause us tremendous pain but it affects the lives of the people around us, passing on the pain we've not been taught to heal. Like the tree in the quote above, we are growing up without roots.

This book exists for two reasons:

1. To give you the skills you need to heal from trauma, overcome depression, and become the strongest version of yourself.

2. I got pissed off.

Let me explain... During the worst years of my depression, I was told that I would have to be on medication for the rest of my life and sit through tens of thousands of hours of therapy with the result of still being triggered, suffering from month-long depressive episodes, enduring suicidal thoughts, and NEVER living up to my fullest potential.

The message was clear: "You are a depressed person, and there's no way out."

Luckily, I grew up in an Italian-American family in Long Island, New York. I grew up with this unnecessarily boisterous attitude that shouted: "No one's going to tell me how to live my life!" So, I fought like hell just to spite these dim-witted idiots. Look, I had no intention of creating a method, helping others, or writing a book—I just wanted to feel good. But, when I discovered one simple reason that men were struggling so much, I had to say something. Plus...I want to spite the people and industry that told me I'd be depressed for good. I proved them wrong, but what if I could help millions of other guys prove them wrong too?

That'd be epic! Let's do it!

The Outcomes of this Book

What you're going to learn from this book is more than just a way out of depression. It's a way to live a more fulfilling and purposeful life as a man.

How?

Think of it this way. Cars all have a similar function: to get us where we're going. They come across different situations. Sometimes, they have to stop quickly, traverse steep terrain, or stick to the road in the rain. Car manufacturers generally equip cars to deal with those situations without malfunctioning or getting into an accident.

But, what if Toyota one day decided that they were going to strip all their cars of effective braking systems and it took the car 30 seconds to come to a complete stop from going 40 mph? That would be insanely dangerous, not just for Toyota owners but for everyone else on the road. This is what has happened to men. Because of the social standards required to be a "man," we've been stripped of our braking systems.

We've been stripped of emotional intelligence, the ability to create healthy support systems, purpose, and self-love, along with the many other qualities required to live a happy, healthy, and successful life on our own terms.

This leaves us almost incapable of navigating a variety of life situations let alone mild to severe trauma. The Courage Method is going to give you the tools that society hasn't so that you can overcome depression. It's stupid simple. Not only that, these same skills will help you achieve the career, relationship, and life goals you're after.

Getting excited yet?

That means by simply practicing the various tools I'm going to give you, you're going to beat back depression and start living the life you've dreamed about. I know you've glimpsed it. You've seen it in moments of clarity when the depressive mind is away and negative self-talk is being held at bay. You can see all that you are capable of being and may even be confused as to why such a powerful person is depressed anyway. I know you truly care about your life and want to be happy. You don't have to go it alone.

Remember, this is your journey. This is your fight. I can give you the tools, methods, and perspectives, but you're going to have to conjure up all the will and courage to go to war. Don't worry... I'm even going to help you with the courage part. My process is called The Courage Method after all.

Alright, to help you win the war on depression and bring that dream from the back of your mind into your life, this is what we're going to do.

1. **Understanding Depression: Discover the Truth about the Depression Trap**

If you haven't pinpointed why you're feeling the way you're feeling, then how can you create a solution? Identifying the problem is the first step in figuring out a solution to depression. We haven't been taught to look at depression in this manner. We'll start by dispelling the chemical imbalance myth to get you clear on the causes of depression. Besides the causes, you'll begin to understand depression as a holistic problem involving your body, heart, and mind. Then, I'm going to have you do some digging. You'll start to examine all of your current moods and emotions so that you can see how they are caused by events or trauma in your past. Then, I'm going to teach you the inner workings of the The Depression Trap so that you have a complete understanding of what's keeping you stuck. You'll be able to use all of these understandings to give you an edge over depression. This section alone will save you years of time on your journey by reframing depression as something that is surmountable.

2. **Fighting Depression: Develop Courage and Habits to put your Healing on Autopilot**

After you've got a complete understanding of what you're up against and a clear idea of what brought you to where you are now, you'll learn to fight. You'll discover that the feeling of courage is more than just a feeling. It's a power that you can develop in your brain. By developing your "courage muscle," you'll be able to overcome feelings of apathy and self-punishing thoughts. The process of developing courage is done through what I call The Warrior's Way, a simple method of building empowering habits that are each designed to combat the physiological and psychological effects of depression. We'll build them like structures in your life, immovable and unshakable. Waging war on depression is a long-term game, so building and layering habits that happen automatically every day are going to put depression's feet to the fire and eventually burn it away. Simple but effective.

3. Learn to Understand, Identify, and Navigate Emotions so that You Can Live a Happier Life and Feel Connected to the People Around You

A lot of the time, for men, this is extremely challenging because we're taught to "man up, shut up, and move on" rather than experience our feelings. We get two options: to be either angry or to laugh. This not only limits our experience of being alive but it makes us more exposed to feeling depressed because of the negativity we've been forced to suppress. Do you think it just magically disappears? No! It lives inside of us, and there's only so much pain and negativity you can hold onto before it starts to turn into depression, anxiety, insomnia, and other life-stealing symptoms. You'll learn how to stop suppressing and start identifying emotions to gain better control over upsets and triggers.

4. Gather Your Party to Go up the Mountain and Slay the Beast

As men, we don't have the support systems that we need to thrive in life. Building a support system will change your life. It's that simple. If it were not for my close family, I'm sure I would have given up and either ended up on the streets or dead. It's sad that we're given the image of a strong man who does it all by himself. Not only does he have the power to do it alone but he must if he wants to be strong, powerful, and essentially...not a pussy. But, I guarantee the people who follow that path feel pretty lonely regardless of their achievements.

If you think of anything that's done in the world, that's great. It happens in groups of people. If you think about the greatest things in the world, like the pyramids of Giza, they weren't built by one person. They were built by hundreds of thousands of people over time. The greatest fighters and Olympic athletes have coaches, and the best musicians and artists have teachers or cohorts. People thrive with other people. I'm going to show you how to gather a party that's crucial to helping you overcome this battle with depression.

5. **Unveil a Practical Idea of "Your Purpose" that Will Serve You Where You're at in Your Life and Drive You Forward**

We're going to talk about purpose on two levels. One as a future burning desire to pull you through this horrific mess—something that's really worth fighting for and that's meaningful and specific to you. We'll also talk about purpose in terms of the present. What's on your plate right now? What aren't you facing? What do you need to focus on? How can we make that a meaningful purpose that you're living for today? Everyone talks about purpose as these airy-fairy big dreams, passion, inborn talent, what you're meant for, and the like, but we're going to develop a different frame for purpose that's much more practical and builds your confidence. You'll be able to use this technique over and over wherever you're at in life and let that drive you forward. Most importantly, it's going to get you laser focused and help you expedite the process of overcoming depression.

Now, I know that sounds like a lot to do, and it might be overwhelming, but if I could sum it up into three very simple points I would say this:

1. Men aren't equipped by this society to deal with their mental health or trauma, and The Courage Method gives you those tools. There's nothing broken about you. You're a car that hasn't been given good brakes. *The Courage Method is* the good brakes.

2. If you follow the method, developing skills, mental models, habits, and support, with continued effort over time, you will overcome this depression.

3. The Courage Method and overcoming depression will build you into a different man. You'll be equipped with everything you need to reach all of your goals in life.

If you don't read any further or you complete this book and throw everything else away, I want you to truly understand this next piece.

Courage is the access to overcoming depression and living a fulfilled life. You don't magically go from sad to happy. You need an emotional transport mechanism. That's what courage is. It is the energy of courage that takes you from one feeling or situation to another. Courage says *"I don't know how this is going to change, but I'm going to go into the unknown, regardless of the fear, and fight anything that stands in my way and emerge victorious."*

My sincere hope is that you read this book and put it into action in your own life and overcome this horrible, life-taking, monster called depression. I want you to know that you don't have to do this alone, and I see you. I understand what you're going through, and if you focus and apply the techniques in this book and you don't stop, you're going to get what you're looking for. I'm just some loud guy from Long Island who figured a way out. I'm turning around, and I'm going to show you the path and help you develop the tools so that you can get out too. I know you have glimpses of a life without this depression and all of the things that you'll do.

So, before you move on to the first chapter, I ask you to do one thing.

Conjure in your mind what you envision your life would be like if you weren't depressed. What kind of relationship would you be in? What would that feel like? What kind of career or job would you be in? How much would you get paid? What would that feel like? What kind of impact would you have on the world? What would you do in your free time as your hobby? What are the hobbies and things that you would involve yourself in? Dream this up real big. I really want you to pull yourself out of the apathy for a moment, put the depression aside, and see what your future would look like without it.

If this brought a little, bitty tear to your eyes, then good. If it didn't and you haven't cried since you were a boy...we'll work on that too!

Now, if you're feeling open, cool. Shoot me an email at dylan@dylanmartinsen.com and tell me what you're seeing. Let me know that you're embarking on the journey to slay the beast. I'll message you back and welcome you to the hardest and best journey of your life. Fight like hell my friend.

You deserve this.

PART I:

Understanding the Journey

"A fly on the window attracted to the light.
His senses are imperfect, so they lead him to his plight.
His life is a struggle now, but his freedom can begin.
If he flies into the dark, and finds the door that he flew in."

—Raymond A Cappo, Shelter

CHAPTER 1:

Life after Depression

How to Read This Book

Before we dive into the depths of The Courage Method, I want to give you a little tiny note on how to read this book. Ready?

Here it is... Just read the book.

I don't want you to go through this book and start implementing the tools and methods I'm going to teach you right away. I don't want you to feel like there's something that you have to do. The reason I say this is because I understand deeply how the depressive mind works. You're going to go into this book and start learning all of these different tools and techniques for overcoming depression, you'll discover new ways to view your life, and you'll get mental models that will change the way you approach your emotions.

There are two routes that the depressive mind is going to go down.

The first route is general apathy about the state of everything. It sounds like: *"This isn't going to work for me... Nothing ever changes... This is B.S."* It's all of the cannot, will not, and won't work talk. That's one route that will derail this whole process. It's like the depression defense mechanism that prevents growth and sabotages your ability to reach your potential.

As for the second route, if you have a particular flavor of self-punishment and negative self-talk, the depressive mind is going to start pointing out everything you've missed, everything you've done wrong. Instead of this book helping you, this part of yourself is going to use it to hurt you, which will end in you abandoning this journey and continuing the cycle of suffering.

This is why I say...just read the book.

I've structured this book in a way that you don't need to get started right away. In fact, in the final chapters, I'm going to give you an outline of your first few steps. There's nothing to immediately implement. There's nothing to fix right now. Presumably, you've been in this place for some time now, so spending a few extra days or weeks (or however long it takes you to read this book) won't be too much longer. Just read this book and allow the new information to start transforming the way you think, feel, and approach your depression. There's no magic about this book other than the fact that I've been through this, I've investigated it, I have a deep understanding of it, and I've laid out the way that I overcame an almost decade-long depression where I went from the brink of suicide to living a happy, fulfilled life.

If you want to begin this journey, just read the book.

Will This Really Work?

So... you might be wondering at this point, "Well, this all sounds well and good, but does this guy have the goods?" I totally get that because the truth is there are a lot of people out in the world who have a lot to say about mental health. "A Simple Method to Overcome Depression or Anxiety." "5 Tips and Tricks to Transform Your Well-being." You know, all those click-bait headlines. Then, you have a lot of therapists or doctors using science-backed research to tell you what to do. This is great, but as with most things, it isn't just what you know. It's your ability to implement it. This is why The Courage Method is different because it's designed for implementation and to build a very practical muscle: courage. In addition, all the other skills (which I refer to as the 3 Arts of Self-Mastery—more on that later) are the science-backed practices, skills, and mindsets that you will build as structures in your life to overcome depression. Hint: it's all the things that we typically don't have as men because of how society expects us to be.

The Courage Method will develop structures in your mind, heart, and spirit that will live with you for the rest of your life. This is not a list of things that you should do that will improve your mental health. It's not some alluring headline in an online article that is going to get your hopes up but then tell you some basic information about dieting and exercise.

The Courage Method contains the exact same structures I've developed in myself over years of trial and tribulation—through horrible, month-long, deep depressive episodes where I spent entire weekends in bed wishing I wasn't alive. I've spent day after day, watching myself in the mirror, lacking the light in my eyes that I once had. I thought about every "wrong" move I made and how I was never good enough, never strong enough, and never successful enough. I felt useless.

What was actually happening during these years of fighting was that I was being forged like hot iron into a sword which transformed me from depressed, purposeless, and unworthy into the strong, confident, and happy man I am today. There's no doubt in my mind that the same transformation is possible for you.

One of the things about depression is that it prevents you from seeing the possibility of what your life could look like without it. I was actually surprised at the person I became after depression. I couldn't even imagine what life would look like without depression, so I want to give you a little peek of what lies on the other side.

1. Happiness without Condition

Obviously, one of the things that you're after is just to feel good. I remember saying this over and over in my head during the years that I was depressed. "I want to feel good." I didn't really care too much about anything else other than finding a way to feel good. It was an amazing transformation just to be able to wake up feeling okay about life—not even happy, or blissful, or excited—just feeling like...everything is okay... It's good.

As you start working with The Courage Method and start healing, you'll no longer be bracing for the next depressive episode. You won't have to endure the dark and sickening thoughts of self-hatred or suicide. When you have a good night out with friends and you're headed home, you won't be living in fear of stepping through the door and the depression returning.

Along with happiness, there's a substance to life that will return to you. Instead of the dull, gray, negative experience you're enduring, you will start to feel life again, the energy of an excited conversation with a friend, the aliveness of standing in a park on a spring day as the breeze moves through the trees, and the excitement of starting a new career, working on a passion project, or just going to stop at the local coffee house. Life will come alive for you.

2. Getting Out of the Fish Bowl

Another thing you can expect to experience as you overcome depression is this idea of getting out of the fish bowl. When I was extremely depressed for those years, I felt like I was in a fish bowl. I was alone and everyone else was on the outside. No matter how close people got to me, or the in-depth conversations that we had, or the eye contact we made—all the things that create human connection—it didn't matter because I was inside and they were outside. I was the one that was covered and clouded with this depression, and even in those "connected" moments, I felt alone. That is one of the most horrible things about depression. No matter how close people are or how much they care, you still feel like you're alone.

After coming out of depression, one of the most beautiful things that I noticed is that I felt connected to people. Now, I can feel more connected to a stranger on the street by sharing a quick "hello" or nod than I ever could when I was depressed with the people that were closest to me.

3. Self-Worth Transformed

All of a sudden, the things in your life start to matter. As your self-worth transforms from the self-hating, internal dialogue to an internal dialogue that has your best interest at heart, you'll start to experience a different world. With a positive, internal dialogue that is supportive, loving, forgiving, and insightful, your view of life will change.

Things in life will matter! Your actions towards other people will matter. The words you speak to the people in your life will matter. The impact that you have at work, in your community, and family will matter. It will matter that you are alive, and you're going to feel that on a very deep level. You'll probably feel that more deeply than people who haven't suffered from depression. It's a blessing and a curse having the full spectrum of going from being dominated by depression to feeling whole and alive. It's a curse because it's a horrible experience to be depressed, and it's a blessing because your empathy will be deeper than most and your resilience will be stronger than most.

4. An Indomitable Spirit

To keep this short and sweet, after you come out the other side of this depression, you're going to be a complete and total badass. Think of it this way. If you can overcome the crippling effects of apathy and depression, there's literally nothing that you can't overcome. Why? By the end of this journey, you're going to have mastered your mind. You're going to be freed from the past that has been holding you back, you'll understand your triggers, you're going to be able release negative emotions, and you're going to know yourself. All of this is going to make you the captain of your ship. You're going to have the confidence to set the destination and overcome any obstacles that come your way, whether they be internal or external.

These are just a few of the benefits that you can expect to receive through using The Courage Method to confront your past and overcome your depression. Even now, I'm discovering new facets of myself and strengths that I didn't know existed when I was in my depressive years. It's like I have a brand new mind, heart, and outlook on life that's helping me achieve all the things that I want out of life. If you take this journey seriously, as your own, as your mission, and as your purpose, I'm sure that you'll join me on the other side.

CHAPTER 2:

The Path of the Warrior

As you know, I'm not a doctor, a psychologist, a psychiatrist, or any -ologist. I'm a guy who went to war on depression and found a pathway that I know would help others do the same.

Let me paint you a picture.

I was on winter break from college, and this holiday season, my depression was getting worse. On Christmas Eve morning, I laid in bed alone thinking about dying. I was not excited about seeing family, not excited about gift giving or receiving, and I did not long for grandma's apple pie. I just thought about how I didn't want to exist anymore and wondered how I could not exist without my family and friends knowing that I even existed in the first place.

I was supposed to go over to my aunt's house for Christmas Eve. It was an all day family hang out, and we're Italian American, so these things are usually big bashes. There's lots of fun, lots of yelling, lots of music, and great food, all served with a heavy dose of sarcasm. Like most people thinking of spending the holidays with family, it was like "Uh oh...here we go." I always knew once we got there, it was going to be a riot, and I loved it. Everyone in my family does something creative: acting, music, cooking, or they've just got some quick wit about them and always have something funny to say. We're not the type of family to have little side conversations and quietly listen to Christmas music. Everyone is involved in everything at all times, and someone always has the spotlight. It's kind of like this unspoken game. Whoever can garner enough attention gets the spotlight. Once you get the spotlight, you'd better perform well or someone is going to sneak in and snag it. It's hilarious, and every Long Island Italian stereotype attends: the grandmother covered in flour and tomato sauce, the uncle that sings Sinatra, the loud cousin that doesn't take shit from anyone, the don-like grandfather sitting silently in the corner, the gossipy aunts – everyone is there.

It's a really good reason to be alive.

But, I laid in bed not wanting to exist. As the morning and afternoon wore on, I started to receive texts from the people in my family asking where I was and when I was coming. I was so ashamed, embarrassed, and apathetic. My aunt asked if I was okay. I answered, "I'm still in bed." Within 15 minutes, she showed up and was sitting on the bed beside me, and not a moment after that, I was bawling.

The pain that I held in my body was overwhelming, and having someone outside my immediate family witness it and be there for me, telling me I was loved—it just opened the floodgates. She held me while I cried for a half an hour. When I started to feel a little lighter, she helped me get ready for the Christmas gathering. I remember spending that day feeling a little ashamed but more held and loved than anything. I learned that I couldn't do this on my own. I could no longer hide my depression to "save face." The truth is...depression is pain suppressed. Everyone has pain, and it's nothing to be embarrassed about or ashamed of. It's just that the societal construct for men is to be this impenetrable statute, to be in control, to be a provider, and to be able to do it alone. Things changed when I started opening up about what was really going on and asking for help.

A week or so later, with the help of my partner, my mother, and my cousin, we called every psychiatry office in a 50-mile radius. Each one had a several-month waitlist and the doctor's offices we called said they wouldn't prescribe anything, not even something as mild as Lexapro.

At that time, we were all under the impression that I could commit suicide, and the overwhelming pain, feelings of emptiness, and hysterical crying fits were unbearable for me and hard on the people I loved. Instead of giving up, we signed into a hospital, the one place I'd never thought I'd end up. You know, I never thought I'd be that person, but there I was, sitting in a hospital mental health ward because the majority of my thoughts were about killing myself. The pain that tore through my heart and body when I imagined the ways I would do it was horrifying, but I didn't have control. It was like something in my brain was feeding me those thoughts.

My mom and my partner came with me, and the main goal was to get medicine and not get put upstairs overnight. That was the last thing I wanted. I just wanted to try taking pharmaceuticals to see if it would give me some kind of relief, so I went through the questionnaire and answered all the questions about my mood and my suicidal thoughts. I re-explained it to the doctor when she asked, and eventually, with a lot of hesitation on their part, we got a prescription. I never thought I'd be happy to be prescribed a depression pill, but I was. It held the possibility that it might make this all go away.

It didn't.

Maybe it stopped me from committing suicide, but it really made me feel more numb and kind of high. I was looking for a solution, not something to soften the blow of the depression; something that could make me feel vibrant and excited about my life. What pushed me over the edge about the whole thing was when I asked the doctor, "How does this work?" She answered, "Well, we don't really know how it works. We just have to keep playing with the dosage and maybe try a different medication."

That's when it hit me.

This person spent years learning how to do something and still didn't know how to do it. Imagine if a plumber came to your house to fix a leak and said, "You know, I don't really know how this works, but I'm just going to try a couple of things. If none of them work, we'll just kind of leave it as is." You wouldn't hire them. That's when I fired my doctor and quit the meds. It was after my experience that I got serious about finding a solution.

I realized that no one was going to come save me. No one was going to care about my own happiness as much as me, even though I was still very depressed and couldn't feel inspired about life. I could still get angry. I was angry that with all the science and knowledge we had as a society, there was no clear route to curing depression. It drove me to try anything and everything to make the dark clouds go away once and for all.

I saw multiple therapists, some really great and some not so great. I did tons of different practices, from martial arts, breathing, meditation, and qigong, to strength training, cold showers, fruitarian diets, herbal detoxes, intermittent fasting, supplements, rolfing, massage, acupuncture, and the list goes on. I tried everything that was said to impact mental health, emotional health, and things that could improve my endocrine and neurological system.

I went on a trial-and-error journey to find the truth.

In this book, I'm going to give you the tools, techniques, and perspectives you'll need to overcome depression. We'll dive into all of it: the truth about courage, the power of surrender, how to build a support system, and everything else I discovered. Remember, this is your journey, your exploration, and a deepening of your wisdom and understanding of yourself. It requires you to do that work, to go into the darkness and return a different man.

Who is This Book For?

If I were to boil it down into demographics, then I'd say this book is for men who are depressed as the result of mild to severe trauma. But really, this book is for anyone that has trauma-induced depression or that is sick and tired of feeling like a victim of their own circumstances. It's for anyone that is ready to be fully responsible for their emotional and mental state or anyone that wants to bring the fire or needs their fire ignited. This is for the man that is ready to dive into the uncomfortable parts of being human and is ready for it to be messy—with epic victories and horrible setbacks.

If you want to develop the courage it takes to relentlessly fight this battle, overcome your worst nightmares, and come out stronger, more resilient, more powerful, and ready to experience life and do things you never thought possible, then this book is for you.

Are you ready to...

- Develop the deep skills to love yourself and forgive yourself so that you can develop confidence and a positive self-image?

- Challenge all the thoughts that you've identified as who you are?

- Uncover all the feelings you've experienced and shoved down because you didn't know what to do?

- Build supportive relationships where you can be open and vulnerable?

These are questions that must be answered because parts of this journey of undoing your depression will feel worse than the depression itself. The apathy will call you back with its sleepy, alluring song, but you must remember that the only way out is through.

While everyone is running around seemingly having a gas, you're working through this mess, developing courage, self-love, support systems, and healthy habits like some nerd. It's not going to feel great...but boy, the man you'll become on the other side—that will be something. You'll be proud of that, and you'll become the person you always knew you could be. Moreover, if you've detected that this trauma is being passed down from generation to generation, you have the opportunity of a true warrior. You will declare that it ends with you, and for generations to come, children will grow up with all the marvelous work you've done without all the pain.

Here's to you. Let's do this!

Before we move on, let's do a short assessment so that you can see where you're at on this journey. This will help you discover the areas where you need the most improvement and others where you might already be doing just fine.

Below, rate yourself on a scale from 1-5 on how accurate the statements are, 1 means "not accurate at all," and 5 means "most accurate." Once you've rated yourself for each statement, total up your scores and then use the Answer Key to determine your next steps.

1. I know what I need to do to improve my mental health.

2. I feel capable of implementing those things to improve my mental health.

3. I have a plan, and I'm ready to get started.

4. I have a strong support system, including family and friends.

5. I am actively working with a therapist.

6. I exercise 3-5 times a week.

7. The exercise I do challenges me physically and mentally.

8. I feel like my exercise regimen is making me a better person.

9. I have a trainer or a coach for the exercise that I do.

10. I eat a mostly whole-food diet.

11. I've researched and tested various supplements, medications, or herbs to improve my mental and emotional health.

12. I seek new ways to improve myself through somatic therapies (examples: massage therapy, acupuncture, chiropractic).

13. I have regular personal and domestic hygiene habits (examples: showering, making the bed, cleaning, and organizing my space).

14. I understand why I am depressed.

15. I understand the life events that caused my trauma.

16. I've identified present situations that trigger depressive episodes.

17. I know the difference between a healthy and a toxic relationship.

18. I can use language to identify various emotional states (example: I can tell the difference between feeling sad, depressed, or regretful).

19. When I have negative emotions, I stay present with them and feel them.

20. I give myself love through affirming thoughts.

21. I can forgive myself for mistakes.

What Your Score Means

Score: 21-50

The Foundations for Mental and Emotional Health Are Missing

Although you want to overcome your depression, there are foundations you need to develop to start seeing the impact of your efforts. You have some understanding of what you could do to improve your situation, but there are still some grey areas. This is mostly due to society's inability to equip you as a man with the core skills needed to navigate emotions and cope with trauma. You will highly benefit from reading Chapter 7. Then, going on to read the rest of the book will point you in the direction of developing the skills you need and building a strong courage muscle to get you through.

Score: 51-75

The 3 Special Ingredients of The Courage Method

If you've landed here, then chances are you've been putting in the work or grew up learning a lot of the skills found in The Courage Method. You may have endured some hard setbacks and might be feeling like it's never really going to change for good. If you're working with a therapist and have built a lot of healthy habits (diet, exercise, and regular personal/domestic hygiene), then I would suggest reading Chapter 7.4 to learn how to dismantle the depression trap and Chapter 7.6 to discover the power of self-love and letting go. Keep going. You got this!

Score: 76+

The War Is Almost Over

You're on your way to overcoming this depression and living a whole new life, but at the same time, you feel like it's never going to end. This is the time to grind it out. The thing about overcoming depression is that it sometimes takes certain experiences to show up in your life. As much as I would like it to be, healing isn't a linear process. It takes time and experiences that you can't necessarily force, but you can do things as a catalyst to induce those healing experiences. This is really the time to start experimenting with various therapies, modalities, and experiences. If you can look back and see the things you've done that made the biggest chances, seek out similar experiences that are going to be a catalyst for your healing. What you need to do now is keep up your momentum. Read the entire book and see if there's anything you've missed. Keep fighting my friend, you're almost there.

CHAPTER 3:

The 5 Hard and Ugly Truths about Overcoming Depression

You might be reading through this book feeling a sense of excitement like a doorway is opening up. That's good, but I'm not going to sugar coat anything on this journey because I want you to be prepared for what lies ahead.

In my heart, I know I can't say that following The Courage Method is going to be an easy process to getting everything you've ever wanted. You're not so naive to believe that either, but it seems like, more than ever, that's the message we're being told by the "people of the internet" that are trying to sell us something.

It's just not the truth of this kind of journey or being human in general. It's confusing, it's challenging, and it can be somewhat tortuous! There are things about trauma and depression that are absolutely horrific...I know you know. There are parts of the journey that are just as horrifying as what you're experiencing now.

What's going to make it easier for you is going into this process knowing what you're in store for, how to identify it when it's happening, and what to do to overcome it. One of the things I wished I had was a road map to getting out of depression when I was clawing my way out. I wanted someone to tell me the way through a certain mountain pass and someone on the other end to cheer me on. When I look back, there were moments on this journey that were epic victories, like going out to a fancy dinner, popping champagne, and regretting the bill type of celebrations. But, I barely knew they were successes! I felt like I just got to a different, more confusing place, or worse, I didn't even realize the progress I was making. My intention is to make your journey a hell of a lot more clear. This chapter might feel like I'm raining on your parade, but I'm just pointing out the danger that lies ahead.

Hard and Ugly Truth #1: Depression Incapacitates the "Oomph" You Need to Escape Its Claws

Depression is *almost* the ultimate catch-22. If you're not familiar, the phrase catch-22 is a paradoxical situation from which an individual cannot escape. The term comes from Joseph Heller's novel, *Catch-22*, where a WWII pilot requests a mental health evaluation and plans to fail that evaluation so he no longer has to fly. However, the psychiatrist deems him fit to return to combat because in making the request, he demonstrated his own sanity.

I say depression is *almost* the ultimate catch-22 because there is a way out, but the mechanics of it are horrible. See, depression, at its core, is *apathy*. Apathy is the belief of "I can't." It's the feeling that we cannot do anything about our situation and no one can help. It is helplessness and hopelessness. To overcome depression, you need some kind of internal force to pull yourself out of it, to take action. But, at the same time, apathy cripples the energy that is required to get out.

What is that force? Courage.

What is another word for apathy? Discourage.

Apathy, as a feeling, as a way of being, and as a mood, hamstrings the exact thing you need to be able to get out of its grasp. It's the antithesis of the remedy. This is exactly why this has been probably the most challenging thing you've come up against. It's the reason that there isn't a clear pathway out. It's literally like asking you to run a race but hog-tying your legs before you start.

The worst part of depression is that no one told you your legs are tied! So, you're left trying to run this race, thinking that it's normal for your legs to be tied. While you're crawling all over the ground, who do you blame?

It's logical for your mind (especially when depressed) to turn around and say, "Okay, I'm depressed and I'm trying to get out, but I'm not making progress. So... there must be something wrong with me." This deepens the negative internal commentary that beats you up. It exacerbates the feeling of hopelessness, and it turns you to darker thoughts that no one wants to hear about.

But the truth is, depression is crippling the exact force you need to get out, and that's courage! This is exactly what The Courage Method is going to train you to develop, like a muscle, so that you can interrupt the whole stress, depress, and self-blame cycle and put it to rest once and for all.

In a few chapters, I'm going to dive deep into the science and power of courage where we'll discuss this multifaceted powerhouse. For right now, this is what you need to know. To combat apathy or discouragement, you're going to need to build up your courage muscle. We'll do that by starting with low lifts and building up to heavier and more challenging feats of "doing stuff you don't want to do but that you know is good for your health," which I believe to be the highest act of self-love.

The Apathy Scale

Alright, let's check in so you can discover for yourself exactly where you are on this journey by simply rating yourself on a scale from 1-5 for each statement below. 1 means "strongly agree," and 5 means "strongly disagree."

1. I don't care about life.

2. No matter what I do, this will never change.

3. Even with someone else's help, I will never change.

If you fell within the 1-5 range, then you're in a deep state of apathy. This is where I was when I fired my doctor and gave up on meds. It was my anger at the system and lack of actual help that got me to go on my journey. Developing courage will help you, but if you've got anger coursing through your blood, a good way to use it is as fuel to fight this war.

If you scored between 6-10, then you're probably still not feeling so great. Maybe you're coming out of that deep state of apathy or your mood fluctuates between apathy and feeling somewhat "normal." Either way, this is the perfect time to cultivate balance and really hone in on building courage with habits I speak to in Chapter 7.5.

If you're on the higher end of the spectrum, from 11-15, then you have a mild, general feeling of apathy, but you're here reading this book for a reason. Oftentimes as men, we struggle to identify how we feel because we've been taught to "man up, shut up, and move on." This ruins our ability to put vocabulary to our feelings while simultaneously silencing us. We're not allowed to talk about our feelings. It wasn't until I went to therapy and started talking about the things that happened to me and how I felt that I realized I had depression. For the longest time, I just thought that was how bad everyone felt. I kept quiet and carried on like I was taught to.

I don't want to project anything on you, but there's a good chance that due to a lack of vocabulary and space to express your feelings, you may be suffering more than you know. This is horrible, but also great news because that means there's a whole world of good feelings ahead of you. Chapter 7.6 talks about this more in depth and how to reclaim your vocabulary and ability to express your feelings.

Hard and Ugly Truth #2: Your Mind Can Keep you Stuck in Depression Instead of Liberating You

I am going to critique talk therapy for a moment, but I also want you to know that therapy is 100% a crucial process in getting through your depression. For me, I saw several therapists in my time, and I still see a therapist every other week for maintenance. Therapy allowed me to have a person outside of my life to check in with on a weekly basis, to explore what actually happened in the past that caused my current condition, and to learn to reframe it for the better. It's an absolute necessity, but I have to put up a huge "CAUTION! DANGER AHEAD!" sign.

What's the danger?

Intellectualization.

Let me be really clear. Therapy is not bad, but the intellectualization of the things you discover can keep you trapped in depression. Your mind is an amazing tool, but when it comes to the emotional part of processing trauma, it's not so great. In therapy, you'll often use your mind to explore the past, identify your triggers, and make the necessary connections to understand why you're depressed. It's an important part of the process of undoing and overcoming depression. You need to understand where all of this pain came from and see how it's influencing you now, but your mind is not going to be able to do the emotional labor that is required to process your past trauma.

It just can't do that.

The mind wants to identify, classify, and, essentially, put everything in their respective boxes, including yourself and your experiences. It will take a deeply emotional and often physical (somatic) experience of trauma and keep it in an intellectual space. Not because the mind is trying to do you dirty but because it's the mind's job to solve problems. That would be fantastic if the solution to trauma was sheerly intellectual, but healing trauma primarily happens in an emotional and somatic space.

I can be a very heady person, and for years, I got caught in the trap of intellectualization. When it came to figuring all of this out, my mind was like one of those detectives with all the pictures, newspaper clippings, and strings connecting all of the dots. I thought that if I just understood it enough, then all of the pain would go away.

But instead, I had a list of justifications for why I felt and acted the way I did. Instead of recognizing that I felt sad, felt pain, felt despair, felt hopeless, felt helpless, and felt scared, my mind chalked all of those feelings up to thinking "I AM DEPRESSED."

There's a very big difference between saying "I am depressed" and "I feel depressed." The first labels things as an emotional experience and suppresses the feeling. The second drops you into a state of recognizing how you feel and gives you the opportunity to be present, to explore it experientially, to shine a light on it, and to empathize and eventually surrender instead of intellectualizing.

For me, instead of finding a way out, I was just looping on this identity and reliving all the horrible things that happened to me. When the past emotions came up, I identified them, labeled them, and suppressed the feelings. For a long time, there was something missing, something to actually transmute the pain from the past, something to help me process it on an emotional and somatic level.

When I discovered the power of surrender, things that weighed on me for years seemingly disappeared overnight. Others took weeks or months of learning to actually be with the emotional experience and surrender to it. I had to learn how to rewire my automatic emotion suppression system that pushed down anything that felt bad.

In this book so far, I've talked a lot about fighting, battling, destroying, and working your courage up to go to war on depression. All of that is required when fighting depression because apathy is such a powerful monster, but the other side of depression is the pain that has been suppressed. You can't go to war on your own pain. You must be with your pain and listen to your pain. You need to understand the past version of yourself that was hurt all those times, all those years ago, and relax, let go, and surrender to let all of that emotion be re-experienced in your body so that it can get out.

Depression is a cleansing of sorts. It's a signal saying to you, *"Hey, I'm in pain. I don't want to be in pain anymore. Stop ignoring the pain."* It takes courage to fight apathy, and it takes courage to feel pain. To heal pain and transmute negative emotions, the mechanism is surrender.

Self-Assessment: Navigating Emotions

For each statement below, respond with either "Yes" or "No" based on your personal experiences.

1. I find it challenging to identify and accurately name my emotions.

2. When faced with a strong emotion, my initial response is to analyze or rationalize it rather than fully experience it.

3. I often use intellectual reasoning to explain away my feelings rather than allow myself to feel and express them.

4. I tend to minimize the importance of my emotions and focus more on logical thinking.

5. Expressing my emotions openly feels uncomfortable, and I prefer keeping them to myself.

6. I frequently find myself saying, "I am [emotion]..." rather than saying, "I feel [emotion]."

7. During challenging emotional moments, I resort to problem-solving rather than embracing the emotional experience.

8. I often use humor or sarcasm as a defense mechanism to deflect from deeper emotional issues.

9. Reflecting on past experiences, I realize I've been more focused on analyzing emotions than fully feeling them.

10. I tend to intellectualize my emotional struggles, believing that logically understanding them is more important than emotionally experiencing them.

How to Score:

Count the number of "Yes" responses to gauge your tendency to intellectualize and avoid feeling emotion. Remember, this self-assessment is not a diagnosis but a tool to help you reflect on your emotional experiences. If you find yourself answering "Yes" to more than five statements, The Letting Go Technique found at the end of Chapter 7.6 will help you identify and surrender to emotional experiences.

Hard and Ugly Truth #3: You Have to Put Everything Aside for Depression

There was a point in my depressive years that I made the decision to put everything aside. I realized that I was never going to reach my life goals if my mental and emotional health was suffering. When I got into relationships, my depression and trauma made them extremely difficult. I couldn't focus on building any type of career that I loved. The creative work I wanted to do was so attached to my self-worth that I couldn't stay consistent because of my negative internal dialogue. There was just no way I was going forward with the huge anchor of depression dragging behind me.

It was hard to make this choice, but once I made it, things started to change.

See, now-a-days, we desire instant gratification. We want the 6-figure job tomorrow. We want tens of thousands of followers on social media. We want our bodies to look a certain way without too much effort. We want to be a stellar athlete or artist that everyone looks up to. Whatever we desire, we want it quick and easy.

The truth is that anything worthwhile, long-term, and impactful takes consistent effort over time. The special ingredient is understanding prioritization.

My grandfather was a general contractor and a custom home builder. He helped clients draft up blueprints of their dream homes then worked with all of his subcontractors to make them come to life. When it comes to building a house, you obviously don't start with the finishings like the doorknobs, light fixtures, paint color, or a fancy jet-bath tub.

You start by digging a hole.

Dig a hole and pour the foundation.

My grandfather would work through the entire process with his team—the excavators, the concrete guys, the framers, the roofers, the electricians, the plumbers, the flooring and tile experts, and the list goes on and on. All of these guys would need to be coordinated in perfect synchronicity to get an empty lot turned into a beautiful home in a matter of months.

Just like building a home, you need to work on the right things at the right time. It might not be the right time to work on relationships or a career. It might not be the right time to start a business. You have to learn to prioritize. Otherwise, it's like trying to frame a house without a foundation. If a house is built on the ground without a foundation, it's going to rot, it's going to shift, the walls and floors will crack, and when a storm comes... say bye bye.

The trouble is, we're being bombarded with a lot of media that tells us all about all the things we have to do and that we have to do them *"right now!"* Whether it's an influencer that wants our attention or a business that wants our money, they probably have their own interests in mind over our own. At some point during this process, you have to evaluate what *you* need to do now. What's going to be the most beneficial thing for you to build now. Is it the finishings, or do you need to start digging the hole for the foundation?

I realized that without my mental and emotional health, I was never going to get the things I wanted in life. Even if I went after them and achieved certain goals, would I ever feel internally satisfied or content? Could it be lasting?

I remember the night I made the decision.

I had just moved to Vermont. I was staying in these "apartments," but it was just an old motel refinished as an apartment complex. I was laying in bed, which was basically in my kitchen, living room, and dining room... You know, because it was actually just a motel room. Law & Order was playing on my tv and I was staring at the ceiling.

Not only was I depressed but I remember thinking, "I don't want to live this life. I don't want my bed to smell like the food I just cooked and pay $1,000 a month for it." I started to look back and think, "What am I doing wrong?" Even though I had been doing some therapy and had been trying to figure out this whole depression thing, I was still trying to go after my dream of being some famous poet, playwright, or novelist. Not only was it stressing me out but it was just a ridiculous thing to focus on while I also wanted to commit suicide. I was trying to install the jacuzzi jet tub when I was living in a tent pitched on an empty lot. I wasn't prioritizing, and I had no idea how to in terms of the entirety of my life path. I was just looking at what I could do in the next few months instead of the next 5 or 10 years.

What if I focused on just digging the hole and pouring the foundation for 1 or 2 years?

First, I tried to plan out the actions in my head. Then, I grabbed a piece of scrap paper and drew a triangle. I put famous writer at the top and worked my way down. On the bottom, I had my mental, emotional, and physical health. Next, I started filling in the actions that I could take to work on those foundational blocks. We'll use this idea later in the book to help you get focused on the right thing at the right time. It will help you not just prioritize the things you should focus on now but it will help you see how digging the hole first is going to help you get all the other things in your life.

Ready to start digging?

Self-Assessment: Exploring Priorities

For each statement, respond with either "Yes" or "No" based on your experience.

1. I often neglect self-care activities that contribute to my mental well-being.

2. My daily routine lacks time for relaxation.

3. I frequently find myself overwhelmed and don't have the time or energy for self-reflection.

4. I avoid reaching out for help whether it's calling a friend or finding a therapist.

5. I use external achievements, such as career success or relationships, as a measure of my overall well-being.

6. I struggle to set boundaries in various aspects of my life, leading to increased stress.

7. My pursuit of goals and achievements often overshadows my focus on mental and emotional health.

8. I rarely make time to do things that bring me joy.

9. I have a tendency to downplay the importance of mental health in comparison to other life priorities.

10. When facing challenges, I lean more towards external fixes than addressing my internal well-being head on.

How to Score:

Remember, this self-assessment is a tool for self-reflection, and there are no right or wrong answers. If you find yourself answering "Yes" to 5 or more statements, it means that you can improve how you prioritize the battle with depression. This doesn't mean you're doing anything wrong. It's just a way of shining a light on where you could better arm yourself for this battle with depression. In Chapter 10, the purpose exercise will help you get clear on what to focus on so that you can start working through your depression.

Hard and Ugly Truth # 4: You Need a Therapist and It's Hard to Get One

Apathy + social standard of masculinity = nightmare.

To get through depression and heal trauma, you absolutely need a therapist, but with apathy and the social standard around masculinity inhibiting you from asking for help, you've got a lot working against you here. Without therapy, I would not have been able to overcome depression and process the trauma I experienced. I was always open to the idea of therapy, but when it came to actually finding a therapist, a whole mess of emotions came up.

Apathy... "This isn't going to help."

Shame... "There is something seriously wrong with me."

Fear... "How am I going to talk about all of this?"

Apathy came from the depression, fear came from the unknown of what therapy was going to do to me, and shame came from who we are taught to be as men: a singular, impenetrable figure who has the ability to deal with everything themselves. Right? If you can't be that singular, impenetrable man who deals with everything themselves, then the result is a feeling of shame, a feeling that something is missing. But, nothing is missing.

That social expectation is really a made up concept of what a man needs to be, and *you* don't have to subscribe to it. You get to define what being yourself means. That social expectation that is hardwired into us is detrimental, not just when it comes to getting a therapist but when it comes to asking for help in general. To complete this journey, you need supportive and positive relationships in your life, and you're going to have to ask for help.

The other part of finding a therapist is sheerly logistical but can be a huge hindrance for most men who need a therapist. Where do you find them? How do you communicate with them? How do you get the right one? How does insurance work? The list goes on. Before I figured out how to do all of this, I cheated myself on the help I deserved. I would say to myself, "I'll do it next week," and then months and years passed before I took action. Then, I'd finally take a look and search around but get discouraged because I felt ashamed for asking if they took insurance or if they could do a sliding scale. Then, there were times when I was working with a therapist but not really getting what I needed, and I stayed with them too long because I was scared to communicate what I needed or to end the relationship. All of these were lessons I had to learn the hard way. With the last therapist I started working with, the whole process from start to the first session (including vetting 4 therapists total) took only 2 weeks and under 2 hours of my time.

Here are a few of the things you'll learn in Chapter 11:

- How to find a therapist within 30 days without stress, overwhelm, or worry.

- How to easily vet your options because they're not all a good fit for you.

- How to draw boundaries, ask for what you need, and end the relationship if it's not working for you.

- How to get your insurance situation worked out or break through the anxiety in asking for a sliding scale price that serves you right now.

So later on, we'll dive into all of the details there so that you can expedite this process and start getting the help that you need. Right now, use the next self-assessment to explore your feelings and potential blocks around finding a therapist.

Self-Assessment: The Fear of Asking for Help

For each statement, respond with either "Yes" or "No" and notice how it makes you feel.

1. I often worry about being judged if I were to share my thoughts and feelings with others.

2. The idea of discussing personal matters with a therapist makes me uncomfortable.

3. I fear that seeking help for depression may be perceived as a sign of weakness.

4. I find it challenging to open up to friends or family about my emotional struggles.

5. The thought of starting therapy feels daunting, and I'm unsure if it would be helpful.

6. I worry about the stigma associated with mental health and seeking therapy.

7. I often tell myself that my problems aren't severe enough to warrant professional help.

8. The idea of vulnerability in therapy makes me hesitant to pursue it.

9. I fear that therapy may bring up emotions or memories that I'm not ready to confront.

10. I downplay the potential benefits of therapy, thinking I can handle my issues on my own.

These questions are designed to get you to look at what's stopping you from finding a therapist. Don't judge yourself. Everyone struggles with this. If you find yourself answering "Yes" to 5 or more questions, pay close attention to Chapter 7.7 on The Art of Help and Chapter 11 for my quick guide for finding a therapist. If you're already seeing a therapist, great work! You will still get a lot of benefit from reading that chapter, especially if you think you could be getting more from the work.

Hard and Ugly Truth #5: It Gets Worse before It Gets Better

When someone violates you and causes trauma, you are the one who has to deal with the impact of it. I feel sick typing that right now because it's so wrong and so unfair. Even if that perpetrator suffered their entire life, were thrown in jail, or were executed, it wouldn't change the mark that was left you.

I'm sorry for what happened to you.

I'm sorry that it's caused so much pain and taken away time that you can never get back. I'm sorry to have to deliver the fifth hard and ugly truth as you start to unearth the pain that lives just beneath your apathy. It might start to feel like it's getting worse. It will feel like you're losing even more time but are headed in the right direction. Your depression will claw at you and attempt to pull you away from this work. It will tell you that trying is useless and that there is no end in sight.

It's not the truth.

I want you to know that every moment you put into overcoming this depression is worth it and that there is a light at the end of the tunnel. I hope this book instills that truth, but I know depression too well. I heard the same sentiment when I was where you are, and I couldn't believe it.

So, I don't expect you to either.

But understand this: depression will have you think in a distorted way. It uses smoke and mirrors to confuse you and deceive you. It will always help you find the negative, not the positive. It will have you interpret situations incorrectly. When someone doesn't respond in a conversation and gets distracted, depression will tell you this person doesn't care. It will minimize the positives in life so that you can't see them. It will tell you that all you feel is depressed, sad, and miserable. It will take one bad grade, one poor remark from an employer, or criticism from a friend and turn it into the most horrible, self-punishing thought.

Depression is the voice that tells you that there is no end in sight and tells you not to believe me. If I were you, I'd put down this book for a moment and ask that voice why it believes that. Check in with yourself before you continue to read. Do you truly believe that? Can you not see a future where you're happy? Can you see it even if it instantly gets clouded by your depression?

It's a scary thing to not be able to believe your own mind, but as you continue to read, you'll be able to distinguish between yourself and the depression more and more. It's going to become more clear as you start to unearth the pain that lives just underneath the skin of your depression. This is going to be one of the most challenging but powerful parts of your process.

By going into those painful situations and emotions and talking about them, whether it's with a therapist, a friend, or journaling, you will bring that pain into your present in a very real way. It's going to cause some significant disturbances, but everything that is built into The Courage Method is designed to hold you through this process. It's everything I wished I had when I jumped head first into the darkness. It's everything I wish I understood about how the depressive mind works. It's all the missing pieces that I had to scrounge around for. It's the mental fortitude required to stay strong on the worst days, and it's the pathway to learning enormous self-love so that you can live a fulfilled life.

That's why I want to share it all with you.

CHAPTER 4:

The Secret Key to Overcoming Depression

You're in a grey room called depression, and relief awaits you on the other side of a locked door. Since we're not given a clear path out, we end up spending a lot of time in that room. We attempt a number of different practices, pills, or otherwise to make the room more comfortable, but at the end of the day, no matter what we do, we're still locked in that room. We give up on getting out because the door is locked and we haven't been given the key.

Courage is that key.

But, what is courage? Is it the poster that we found plastered up in our high school? Is it *just* a word that politicians use when sending men to war? Is it a mysterious force that possesses us in times of danger?

Warriors, artists, activists, athletes, politicians, and people have used the word courage for thousands of years to explain a feeling that rises up within us. It tells us that something is coming, some kind of challenge, and that we must resist it. We must fight it. We've observed that courage is stronger in some than others. While some rise to the challenge as that feeling courses through their bodies, others turn and run and never experience the "magical" force of courage. Is it inherent in some and not others? Can you strengthen and practice courage? Does it arise from the ethereal spirit, or is it something more biological?

All questions will be answered, but first, I want to be clear about something. When I started writing this book, I began with my experience of overcoming depression. I did not understand why what I did worked. I had no structures or frameworks. All I had was a list of everything I did and my thoughts on their efficacy. In the process of writing this book, I knew that in order to be helpful, I needed to build something. I didn't want to write a memoir about my horrible experiences and how I felt better at the end. I wanted to create something that you could take and apply to your own life. That's what you're reading right now.

In the early stages of getting out of depression, something I noticed about my experience was that I just kept fighting no matter what happened. It was the main driver behind my success, and I also noticed, especially in the final stretch, that this quality of fighting became even easier to access. Like a battle-hardened warrior, I was always ready to dash into battle and still am.

The only thing I could call it was courage.

After identifying that mechanism, I was concerned that this was something singular to me because of my martial arts training. What if I spent all of this time and wasn't able to give you something that would really work? That's when I stumbled on the science that corroborated my experience in one of those odd, synchronistic moments that life often brings.

Recent studies allow us to pinpoint the seat of courage, usually referred to in research as tenacity, willpower, or grit. It's not a magical or mystical force bestowed upon a lucky few. We've learned that there is a structure in the brain that is responsible for generating that feeling of needing to resist or fight. What's more, we're learning that, with practice, that part of the brain can grow and become more easily activated. Courage can be developed almost like a muscle.

Science Revealed: The Anterior Mid-Cingulate Cortex

The anterior mid-cingulate cortex (aMCC) is a part of the brain that lights up when a person has an experience of courage or willpower. In one study, researchers stimulated this part of the brain and asked participants about the feelings they experienced. One participant noted, "It's as if there is a storm off in the distance. I know I need to go into the storm, and I know I can make it through the storm."

Sounds like courage, right?

When comparing this scenario with a control group where participants' anterior mid-cingulate cortexes weren't actually stimulated, participants reported a lack of that sensation. This emphasizes that this part of the brain does have an impact on the feeling of what we call willpower or courage. The aMCC is where the feeling and intent of "I absolutely will" arises from. It's the powerhouse that allows us to overcome and to fight. In additional studies, it was also found that the aMCC lit up when participants resisted something they wanted. Courage is not just the intent of "I absolutely will" but it's also the intent of "I absolutely will not."

Through imaging studies, scientists also discovered that the activity in the aMCC is significantly lower in individuals that express apathy or are diagnosed with major depressive disorder.

That makes sense, right?

When we're depressed, we lose our fight, we give up, and we don't care. We literally lose our *will* to live. Now, if you're thinking, "I knew there was something wrong with my brain," hold your horses. I don't believe that this is saying there is something broken in your brain. Rather, this part of the brain could be functioning normally; it's just not being activated because of depression.

This leads to the question... How?

I believe there is a moment we all have during or in the wake of a traumatic experience, a moment where we give up and where our will to fight gives out because whatever we are going through is too overwhelming, too dark, and too painful. Instead of continuing to fight, we give in to apathy, the deep-rooted belief "I can't." This is why I suggest developing your courage muscle as a solution to overcoming depression—and it's actually possible.

In yet another study, researchers had two groups perform exercise regimens 3 times a week. The first group had to do 60 minutes of moderate to high-intensity cardio, and the second group had to do 60 minutes of light aerobics. They compared their aMCC images after 6 months. The group that had to do the moderate to high-intensity cardio had increased activity and a larger aMCC, whereas the other group remained stagnant. Why? Well, when investigating further, they found that the cardio group was significantly more challenged by the exercise intensity, whereas the aerobics group was not.

Are you picking up what I'm putting down?

Every time we do something where we have to overcome resistance, we activate the anterior mid-cingulate cortex. The more often we do that, this part of our brain strengthens, so to speak. Then, it becomes easier to activate this part of our brain and access the feeling of tenacity or courage.

It's kind of a like a muscle growing, and this is how it happens:

Step 1: Activate

Engage in activities that require overcoming resistance, like facing fears, pushing physical limits, or fighting through any challenge. This activates the aMCC and initiates the neural processes associated with courage and willpower.

Step 2: Practice

Regularly expose yourself to situations demanding courage or willpower. This could include regular exercise, tackling difficult tasks, or embracing discomfort. The repetition reinforces the activation of the aMCC and develops it's ability to activate.

Step 3: Adapt

Over time, the aMCC adapts to the increased demand for courage and willpower, growing in size and developing greater neural connections.

Step 4: Enhanced Access

As the aMCC strengthens and grows, accessing feelings of courage or willpower becomes more natural and automatic. The enhanced neural infrastructure allows for quicker and more efficient activation of willpower and courage.

Courage: The Key to Everything

Let's wrap this up.

You're starting to put all the pieces together, but if you want to understand how courage can help you overcome depression, then we need one final piece: the basic understanding of how a person makes change happen in their life. This might sound kind of obvious as we go through it, but bear with me. It's important.

Here's an example. Paul wants to lose 10 lbs to reveal his shredded core. To get to that goal, Paul is going to have to alter his behavior. Since these are behaviors he's not doing already, there is going to be resistance there.

Simple, right?

Wherever there's resistance, there's an opportunity to grow. Let's say that to lose those 10 lbs, Paul needs to start doing a new exercise regimen four times a week. If he does the exercise, he can lose the weight. Let's call that taking action. "Doing something you don't want to do to achieve a desired result."

Similarly, to lose those 10 pounds, he needs to stop eating six cheeseburgers a week. There's resistance there because if there was no resistance there, he would've stopped eating the cheeseburgers and he'd be at his goal weight. Very similar to the first half of this example, right? But, it's a little different. Let's call that resisting action. "Not doing something that you want to do to get the desired result."

You can see that these points of resistance are the points where change happens. If Paul follows through on his plan, not only will he get the external results but something even better is happening—he's building his courage muscle. Over and over, he's overcoming the resistance he feels to exercising, and he's resisting the urge to eat cheeseburgers.

We come to the conclusion that courage and willpower is the powerhouse to creating change in your life. It gives you the ability to take action, "Doing something you don't want to do to get the desired result," and resist action, "Not doing something that you want to do to get the desired result." Just think about anything that you desire in life. There's always resistance, right?

If you develop your aMCC, built your courage muscle, then anything is possible. And honestly, since you're going to be starting this journey in the depths of depression—on the exact opposite spectrum of courage—the strength that you'll build in your courage muscle will be incredible. They say your greatest weakness in life is set to become your greatest strength. It's because you have to deeply understand it, you have to work for it, and your have to fight against it. If apathy is your greatest weakness, then courage will become your greatest strength—it just may be your destiny.

Putting Courage in The Courage Method

Unfortunately, you're not going to read through this book and instantly walk out with a better ability to access courage unless, of course, you have no desire to read this book and it's a huge challenge to read it. Then, you'll be developing courage! Courage is not created without action. It requires that you, just like Paul, take action, "Doing something you don't want to do to get the desired result," or resist action, "Not doing something that you want to do to get the desired result."

In Part II of this book, I'm going to reveal a special method, The Warrior's Way, for developing your courage muscle so that you can use it to overcome depression. Courage is the antithesis of apathy, and it's the a core requirement to empower and access the other tools, techniques, and mindsets you will learn throughout this book. Here's a brief overview of that relationship.

Purpose

We're going to reframe purpose. Not as the heavy thing you need to figure out so when someone asks, "What's your passion?" you have a nice, ready-made answer. The Courage Method's purpose is much more flexible and practical. I'll break it into two different types of purpose. You must develop a long-term purpose, which is the desires that will pull you into the future, things that will get you excited to be alive. Then, there's your purpose right here and right now. Right now, you have a little less control over this because your purpose right now is dealing with depression. The reason it's structured in this way is because most people are going to want to ignore the thing that is causing them pain and move on to the "fun stuff." Dealing with what is at hand will get you where you're going faster, especially if it's something uncomfortable. Confronting depression and exploring your pain will requires enormous amount of courage and willpower. It's exactly what you don't want to do, and there will be many moments where you'll want to quit. That's a feeling you'll most certainly need to resist.

Understanding

Understanding embodies everything from emotional awareness and compassionate introspection to self-love and letting go. These are skills that you will build throughout The Courage Method. The core of what these skills will offer is the ability to navigate your emotions and your past. It's like having a torch in a dark cave. You'll learn to identify what you feel, why you feel it, how to communicate it, and how to let it move through you. There's a lot of rewiring that goes on while you build these skills. The need for courage arises when you need to resist the impact of a trigger. Do you fly into an uncontrollable rage? Do you dissociate and head to bed for the day? Whatever it is, you'll learn to identify and resist the automatic actions that your brain has set in stone so that you can instead be present with the pain and those feelings and take a new action.

Support

I've said it a few times and I'll say it again. No one gets through trauma and depression alone. I'm going to show you the exact people that you need around you to get you through this. For most guys, it's a lonely world out there. Men over 30 have fewer friends and spend less time out with friends than they have in the last 50 years. This indicates that there are blocks around building healthy relationships. Building this support network is going to take your out of your comfort zone in terms of vulnerable communication, drawing boundaries, and bringing these people into your life, but you're going to use your courage muscle to do it and have a support system that will help you navigate this adversity. Plus, it will all feel a lot less lonely.

Habits

The Warrior's Way is a method for building healthy habits in your life that will improve your overall physical, mental, and emotional health. Everytime you add one of these habits, you're going to consistently have to either take action or resist, further developing courage. I'm going to give you the core habits you need to build to grow your courage muscle and support your mental health.

We'll start slow so that you can build your courage muscle and practice for overcoming even bigger monsters. For example, when you get triggered, even though it doesn't feel like it, you have a decision to make. Do you stop and feel the horrible feelings that come up? Do you have the presence of mind to do some deep breathing? Does the trigger take you away and bring you down a normal path which ends in a depressive episode and self-punishing thoughts? That's the real battle. When you develop courage in The Warrior's Way, you strengthen that muscle so that when the trigger comes up, you're more prepared to overcome something that almost feels impossible to overcome.

What's more, what about going to therapy and bringing up those old traumas and those old pains? No one wants to do that. No one wants to feel those feelings. No one wants to relive that pain. It takes an enormous amount of courage to do that work. That's why we train courage as the core of this methodology because courage is the secret key to everything.

It's the key to undoing your triggers and taking back your life. It's the key to uprooting the past and reliving the pain you experienced and having a space to surrender and release that pain.

It's the key to authentic happiness.

If this sounds like a lot of time and effort, then know that none of this is wasted. Courage is also the key to becoming the man you want to be. See, after overcoming depression, the biggest battle of my life, the courage and willpower I have is extraordinary. Not only have I built it as a structure into who I am but all the skills, abilities, habits, and relationships are all the things required for success in this world. So, if you feel like, "Wow, this sucks that I have to spend years of my life doing this," reframe it. You're spending time building the foundation you need to succeed and create a future that is worth fighting for. After this is through, you'll be more equipped than you ever have been to navigate your own emotions, relentlessly follow your passion or career, have deep, fulfilling relationships, and of course—*feel good*.

You're not going to walk out of this experience the same person that you are today. You're going to feel different, you're going to think differently, you're going to act differently, and you're going to go after things that you never thought were possible.

It starts with building courage... an indomitable spirit.

CHAPTER 5:

The Catch

In the last few chapters, we've discussed what life looks like after depression, the hard and ugly truths about the journey, and the main driving force behind The Courage Method.

Before you embark on this adventure, I want to leave you with one last piece of wisdom. It's about setting expectations and setting up your approach.

At the onset of achieving any goal, people do a few things to prepare. They ensure that it is something that they truly want. They make sure that they have the time and energy to take it on. They usually have some kind of plan or method to get there.

What is often ignored is setting expectations and learning to approach it in the right way.

I don't want you to jump into this, full of excitement and energy, but when you hit your first road block be totally deterred and give up. It's easy for that to happen with depression.

What can prevent that?

Getting clear about your expectations and how you're going to approach this process. After reading the first few chapters, I want you to check in with yourself to see what you've got so far.

Can you see a pathway starting to emerge?

Are you feeling excited, or are you scared?

Do you think this whole process is going to go smoothly?

How long do you think this is going to take? A month? A year?

Do you think this is a good solution for you?

There's no wrong answer here. Of course, you may not have answers to all of these questions, and doing this short check-in just may have created more questions! All will be answered in time. There are two things you need to know before you read on.

1. The Courage Method is not a short-term fix.

2. You're not a lawn mower.

Let's deal with the first one. The Courage Method is not a short-term fix. In our culture, people want the easy pill solution to any problem that arises. It's just the way that we often approach problems in this fast-paced world. We want to move away from pain and get back to feeling good as fast as possible.

Here's an analogy:

Mary walks into the doctor's office holding a burning hot pan. She's not just holding the pan by the handle. Her other hand is on the skillet. She's crying out in pain. She says, "Doctor! Doctor! You have to get rid of this pain for me!" The doctor looks at her and says, "Oh yes, it looks like you are in a lot of pain from holding that hot pan." The doctor takes out his prescription pad and writes her a prescription for a painkiller and sends her on her way.

This is generally how we deal with pain in our society, by suppressing it.

The pain in Mary's hand is a symptom of the actual problem. The problem, which is pretty clear in this example, is that her hand is on a hot pan. The Courage Method is different in its approach for dealing with pain, so it will not be as easy as taking a pill.

For the most part, our society is going to tell you to go and take a pill to fix the chemical imbalance in your brain. I wish depression was that simple. I wish it was that easy. I wouldn't have to write this book and a lot of people would be a lot happier if so, but that's simply not the truth of depression. All of the apathy, self-hating thoughts, and debilitating depressive episodes is just like Mary's burning hand. It's a symptom of the actual problem. In other words, it's the body communicating, "YOUR HAND IS GETTING BURNED!" The Courage Method is designed to guide you in dealing with the actual problem—suppressed pain. Instead of telling you to take a painkiller, I'm going to walk you through the process of taking your hand off the pan to stop the burning once and for all.

So, when I say this is not a short-term fix, what I mean is that this process is not going to take a few weeks or even a few months. This process could take a year or more. Why? Not only do you have to confront the suppressed pain of trauma but it's going to take time to arm yourself with the tools that society has stripped from you as a man. You're going to have to learn all of these new things while you're healing from your trauma and pain.

Now, the second one. You're not a lawn mower; you're a human. A lawn mower is simple to fix for a few reasons. We know everything about lawn mowers. There are manuals for lawn mowers. We know how they work because we built them.

You, on the other hand, are a unique, biological human being with a unique life experience. You're not a lawn mower built on an assembly line. We don't yet know how all of the insides of us work. We did not build humans. There is no manual for fixing humans.

What I'm trying to say is that this healing path is not linear, and it's not always clear.

You must approach it like that.

The Courage Method is going to give you a framework and replace a lot of the tools you've been stripped of by society, tools you need to overcome depression and heal your trauma. It's going to give you perspectives that you've never had before.

You must approach this process with a curious nature. This is really a journey of deepening your understanding of being human...and being yourself.

I want you to think of this as your hero's journey.

In every hero's journey there is...

- A party you must assemble to support you in your journey.
- Training you must do to prepare your body, heart, and mind.
- A foe that must be beaten.
- A transformation as a result of all the hard work you've done.

In the next part of this book, I'm going to give you everything you need to go on this journey, to gather your party, go up the mountain, slay the dragon, and come back a different man. Everything that is going to happen on that journey is going to be unique to you. There will be things you discover that I could never know to put in this book. There will be darkness that you confront that only you will ever be able to speak to. There will be great joys and triumphs and there will be devastating defeats, but if you dedicate yourself to this journey and use The Courage Method as your guide, you will, with continued effort, come back down that mountain with a smile on your face.

Ah, yes. I almost forgot. There's one more element that is required in every hero's journey.

A call to action.

This is that.

Will you heed the call?

PART II:

The Courage Method

> "You gain strength, courage, and confidence by every experience in which you really stop to look fear in the face. You are able to say to yourself, 'I lived through this horror. I can take the next thing that comes along.'"
>
> —Eleanor Roosevelt

CHAPTER 6:

The Warrior's Way

Welcome to Part 2 where I will finally lay out The Courage Method in its entirety, step by step. We'll start by understanding the core mechanism that will help you build your courage muscle: The Warrior's Way. As we discussed earlier, courage is the power behind The Courage Method. Not only does it fuel The 3 Arts of Self-Mastery revealed in Chapter 7 but it's the antithesis of apathy and the key to overcoming depression.

The Warrior's Way is a habit-building method for developing your courage muscle so that you can overcome the challenges you're going to face on your journey of healing from your trauma and overcoming depression.

What it is and Why it Works

One of the missteps that many people make when getting out of apathy and depression is trying to feel good. This makes total sense as a reaction to depression. They want to be able to go from a deep state of depression and jump right into being happy. They want to get away from it and run.

But, you need something in between to transport you to those higher emotional states. You need something to break through the apathy, something to ride on the coattails to pull you out of the place of desperation that you're living in, which is exactly why we focus on courage. Courage is that vehicle. Dr. David Hawkins' Map of Consciousness illustrates this perfectly. In his Map of Consciousness, you'll find that apathy (or depression) is one of the lowest emotional states and peace and joy are some of the highest emotional states. Courage is found right in the middle. In fact, courage is the bridge between all the lower, negative emotional states and the higher, positive emotional states—not just apathy and joy.

Try to think back to the last time you were in a deeper depressive episode. How did you get out? Were you lying in bed, and did it all of a sudden disappear, going from apathy and suffering to joy and peace?

Probably not.

Whenever I look back on my experience, there was a feeling of courage between my apathy and the moment I was able to take an action. I got out of bed and took a shower, went to the gym, or cleaned the house, or I was able to let the deep pain through and cry it out.

Name of Level	Energetic Log	Predominant Emotional State	View of Life Is	View of Life	God-view	Process
Enlightenment	700-1000	Ineffable			Self	Pure Consciousness
Peace	600	Bliss	Perfect		All-Being	Illumination
Joy	540	Serenity	Complete		One	Transfiguration
Love	500	Reverence	Benign		Loving	Revelation
Reason	400	Understanding	Meaningful		Wise	Abstraction
Acceptance	350	Forgiveness	Harmonious		Merciful	Transcendence
Willingness	310	Optimism	Hopeful		Inspiring	Intention
Neutrality	250	Trust	Satisfactory		Enabling	Release
Courage	200	Affirmation	Feasible		Permitting	Empowerment
Pride	175	Scorn	Demanding		Indifferent	Inflation
Anger	150	Hate	Antagonistic		Vengeful	Aggression
Desire	125	Craving	Disappointing		Denying	Enslavement
Fear	100	Anxiety	Frightening		Punitive	Withdrawal
Grief	75	Regret	Tragic		Disdainful	Despondency
Apathy	50	Despair	Hopeless		Condemning	Abdication
Guilt	30	Blame	Evil		Vindictive	Destruction
Shame	20	Humiliation	Miserable		Despising	Elimination

Spiritual Paradigm: Enlightenment–Love
Reason & Integrity: Reason–Courage
Survival Paradigm: Pride–Shame

It didn't magically transform my experience into sheer bliss, but it allowed me to get out of apathy and start moving upward. I activated the courage muscle then used that energy to go do something that was good for my health.

This principle applies not just to those singular moments but also to the journey of overcoming depression as a whole. Courage is the vehicle to escape from moments of despair, but it's also the vehicle to escape from the multi-year mood of depression. Before we get into using courage to pull you out of deep depressive episodes, we need to train courage.

If you chose to heed the call to adventure in the last chapter, then the next phase of a typical hero's journey is meeting the mentor that offers wisdom, guidance, and training to overcome the enemy. Just think of the training montages in kung fu films where the kung fu master trains the young hero. He runs up and down the mountain everyday, does thousands of kicks, stands in a deep horse stance with a staff and two buckets of water over his shoulders, and finishes his day in a dark hall throwing punches at candle flame.

The Warrior's Way is that part of your hero's journey to develop your courage muscle for the battles that lie ahead.

Now, those battles aren't slaying a dragon or stopping the rule of an evil regime. We're talking about the battle of going from apathy and depression into the pain of the past to confront the awful things that happened so that you can process, surrender, and release yourself from the pain that's causing this depression. We're talking about real situations in relationships with friends, parents, or lovers when someone sets off one of your triggers and you want to run away, shut down and dissociate, or shout out in anger.

Instead, you'll be able to acknowledge and understand what's happening and be with the pain that arises from that trigger—that's what you're being prepared for. We're preparing you to hear all your thoughts, feelings, and reasons why you don't want to get a therapist but go get one anyway because it's proven to help. These are the battles that lie ahead, and I'm going to guide you through all of that.

When I reveal how to deploy The Warrior's Way in your life in the coming chapters, you might think, "The Warrior's Way looks like you're just building habits." It's true that we are going to be building habits, but we're actually going to be doing two things simultaneously.

1. We'll build habits as a way to develop your courage muscle.

2. We'll build habits into your life that improve your mental, emotional, and physical health.

It's designed that way on purpose. During my martial arts training, which we'll talk about in a moment, I didn't just focus on martial capability. It was a complete system that included dieting, exercise, meditation, philosophy, and martial arts. The Warrior's Way develops habits that directly influence your physical, mental, and emotional state while challenging you so that you can grow your courage muscle.

Why do one thing just to develop courage when you can bind the two together with practices that science has proven will help improve your overall mental, emotional, and physical wellbeing? This will help combat the suffocating nature of depression.

How I Discovered The Warrior's Way

We have to start at the beginning, but I won't belabor you with all the details of my life. I'll share just enough to show you how I ended up where I did and the why behind The Warrior's Way. Growing up, there was financial instability in my household, my parents got divorced, and my father was almost debilitated with Lyme disease. That instability forced me to grow up really quickly, and I made some decisions about who I was in the world.

1. I had to take care of the people around me.

2. My parents' experiences, thoughts, and feelings needed to be prioritized over my needs.

3. Who I was or what I needed wasn't important.

This tanked my confidence and self-worth and made it hard for me to express my feelings because I didn't want to be a burden to my parents' already hard and confusing lives. All of this left a lasting imprint on how I interacted with myself, the people around me, and what I thought of myself—which wasn't much.

Eventually, in my teen years, my depression started to become apparent. At first, it was hard to identify because it was normalized as my experience of life—I thought everyone felt that way. But, when I was first exposed to meditation, I started to become aware that something was wrong. I began to read dozens of books on spirituality and eastern philosophy, which pointed towards this path of relieving past emotional pain to transform the present. Of course, the western new age spiritual books had a bit of a spin on it, not just to transform your life but essentially how to get more stuff. That's a rant for another day. Anyway, I was able to acknowledge that what happened in my life contributed to the negative relationship I had with myself. That pain manifested as depression, anxiety, unhappiness, a lack of confidence and self-esteem, and all of the negative qualities that held me back. I knew I needed to confront this within myself if I wanted to be happier.

This path led me to going to school for massage therapy after graduating high school where I met my first kung fu teacher, or sifu, in my early 20s. I had always wanted to study martial arts but didn't have the confidence to go and do it. This was the perfect time and the perfect setting. Not only did I learn martial application but there was a focus on the transformational aspects of the arts which entailed hard physical training, meditation, and qi gong (breath work). My sifu not only taught me martial arts but he led me to something within. He gave me methods for strengthening my will and healing my past in a VERY visceral and practical way.

Building an Indomitable Spirit

A typical day training kung fu wasn't anything typical when it came to most martial arts programs, let alone most exercise programs. We trained outside, rain or shine, in winter or summer, and the training was intense.

The training always began with a myriad of push-ups that included presses on the knuckles, back of the wrist, 5 finger, 3 finger, 2 finger, and more. It was hard enough doing them on the hard earth, but overtime, I graduated to doing them on gravel, brick, and the most intense: brick topped with bits of fine gravel. With my belly to the earth, I dragged myself across the ground in an exercise called "drag palm" with an array of different hand positions designed to strengthen the back, chest, palms, and elbows. We did frog hops and duck walking, which were full body jumping and squatting exercises to strengthen the legs and to develop hip power. These are just a few of the hundreds of conditioning exercises and forms I did during my training. There were no reps or sets. Everything was done to exhaustion and then a little more.

Every day of training was hard. It never got easier, and it was designed to be that way. There was intention behind the intensity. The core intention was to learn to be present and learn to let go. The intensity of the training brought past emotional pain and trauma to the surface. It challenged the mind and revealed weaknesses. The remedy to everything that it revealed wasn't to become harder but to let go of the pain and the attachments to the past. It was a very intense and healing time in my life. The training provided an emotional catharsis which allowed all of the suppressed pain to flow out of my body, heart, and mind.

It taught me to develop present moment awareness in the most intense conditions, whether it was freezing water or gravel pressing against my knuckles. It wasn't a way to ignore pain but to accept the pain of life, learn to be with it, and surrender. When you are able to be at peace with discomfort or pain, override the mind's desire to stop, and keep going in that type of training—it changes you for life.

My sifu called it building an indomitable spirit. He would say that in life, and in a fight for your life, you want to be able to overcome fear and pain, and the best martial artists were able to keep getting up no matter what. It was developing the spirit inside to overcome internal and external circumstances. It was the development of the courage muscle that gave me the ability to go to war with depression and overcome the unrelenting emotional apathy and self-hating thoughts. That is the same courage muscle I'm going to instruct you to build for this battle.

Now, if you're reading this imagining a man yelling at me while I brutalized my body—that's not it. My sifu would always gently say "keep going" when we were doing the most brutal trainings. When I couldn't do one more press and my arms were shaking uncontrollably with sweat pouring down my face—keep going. When I was hanging upside down from a tree with my legs wrapped around a branch, holding on with by only interlocking my feet—keep going. When I was standing in a deep horse stance for 30 minutes with a staff and buckets of water on my shoulders—keep going.

Whether you want to call it developing an indomitable spirt or developing a powerful anterior mid-cingulate cortex, well, that's up to you. I was growing my courage muscle, my ability to see and feel the adversity, fear, or pain…and keep going. This training was extreme. I'm glad I experienced it, but it's not for everyone nor is it required to build an "indomitable spirit" or courage.

The Warrior's Way that I'm going to share with you is designed to build that same voice within you. When it gets really hard, really terrible, really dark, and really painful…just keep going. Overcoming depression is not as complicated as most would make it seem. If you can *keep going*, you will get out of this. With that mentality—along with an open mind and the tools in this book—you'll be good to go.

CHAPTER 7.1:

The 3 Arts of Self-Mastery

If this whole process feels daunting, know that that's just part of the process. I've said it before and I'll say it again: this path is more than just about overcoming depression. This is a journey of self-mastery. It's the greatest weapon that you have against depression, and it's one of the best things you can do for every other area of your life.

It will start with uprooting this depression. First, you'll learn how depression moves and how to fight back with the *Art of War*. Next, you'll learn the *Art of Help*, how to build a network of people around you to support yourself in overcoming depression. Finally, you'll learn how to deepen your emotional awareness, identify feelings, develop self-love, and neutralize past pain through surrender with the *Art of Alchemy*.

These arts will give you everything you need to heal trauma and overcome depression. In this process, you'll learn to master your mind and emotions but also learn to give yourself a damn break and a lot of love. This is the exact opposite of what we've been taught: cynicism, resignation, isolation, and emotional suppression.

After uprooting depression, The 3 Arts of Self-Mastery offer a completely different life than how most live. You'll start to choose the right friendships and romantic relationships that are supportive and drama-free, you'll find a career or start a business that brings you joy and wealth, you'll navigate challenging situations with ease and be able to draw boundaries when needed, you'll lay self-hate to rest, and your life will turn from chaos to peace.

These three arts are in fact arts—meaning, they are personal to you and take time to learn and develop. For example, let's take the journey of a painter from newbie to great artist. That person must first learn some kind of techniques for how to use and move the various brushes, they must learn how to mix paints, and they must be familiar with the different types of paints and canvases they can use. Over time and with practice, these techniques become personalized and unique to them—they develop their own flavor. Eventually, they create their own techniques and perhaps even pass them on.

The 3 Arts of Self-Mastery have both understandings and techniques. You must take them and start to use them by applying them to your everyday life. Some may click instantly and others may be more challenging. To gain self-mastery, you must practice. You must study the techniques and yourself. There is certainly a way to do this, but don't get caught in trying to do it the right way. You find that by doing and reflecting. Eventually, these arts will be yours, personal to you and your experiences, and you'll develop your own techniques. Since you are unique, I cannot give you all the answers for what is going to work for you. As you develop a deeper understanding of yourself and your condition, you'll develop your own ways of practicing these arts.

Final thing before we dive right in.

In Chapter 9, I will reveal a 4-phase process for practicing these arts in your life. So as you're reading about the arts, don't worry about the how and when. Focus on the arts, understanding them, feeling them in your heart and body, and letting them start to change your mindset and perspective, and write down any insights you may have.

The Art of War

"It is easy to love your friend, but sometimes the hardest lesson to learn is to love your enemy."
— Sun Tzu

CHAPTER 7.2:

Understanding Depression

The first part of *The Art of War* is understanding depression, and the second part of it is fighting depression where you'll learn The Warrior's Way. Before you're truly able to defeat any enemy, you need to understand your enemy: how it moves, how it deceives, and how it fights. There are many layers to depression that most do not understand, especially people who haven't experienced it, let alone overcome it. This chapter is dedicated to giving you a time to understand, investigate, and explore depression.

It's true that depression is a monster. It's true that you must fight against it to overcome it. It's true, too, that under the layers of depression is a tangle of emotions that need to be heard, understood, and loved.

You feel that on some level, right?

You tell yourself that you don't care, and you want it all to end or feel the pressure just behind your eyes and heaviness in your chest. There are times when you fake a smile and say, "It's all good," wishing someone would prod just a little further.

It's all there.

But, what's just underneath the surface feels so hideous and dark that if let out, it could consume life itself, right?

It's all the versions of yourself that hold the pain of every heartbreak, every betrayal, and every fear you were taught to push down. Me, you, and maybe billions of men throughout time have done just that, and we've done a damn good job. That's the thing about being a guy. If you're given a blueprint to follow, a linear way to do something, and you're drilled on it, we can be damn good at it because we like doing well. Every discomfort, fear, worry, and feeling that came across our radars we shoved down *just* like we were taught.

But, that horrible darkness still cries to be let out. As the months and years wear on, we just become more numb, confused, disassociated, further from who we thought we'd become, and angry.

That anger sometimes comes out to the people we love but often as a self-punishing voice that tears us apart. It judges everything we do, tells us we want to die, and hates every fiber of our being. It's anger, but it's a voice that's inside you but not really you at the same time.

Have you ever gotten that feeling when you hear that voice for a moment and think, "Is that me? Who is saying that?" and it returns with some horrid remark, covering its tracks so that you're duped into thinking that, "yes," that is in fact how YOU feel about YOURSELF.

This is one of the many confusing problems about depression, and in this chapter, I'm going to reveal to you every little thing I undercovered about the truth of depression. I'm going to show you that, in this strange way, you do need to do battle with depression and fight for your life. But simultaneously, overcoming depression is about feeling, understanding, and learning to love yourself. It might not be what you want to hear. It might not be something that you get or know how to do right now, but I know that if you understand the inner workings of depression, if you understand its tricks and deceptions and understand the truth of it—you're going to be able to really start making some progress. Like I said earlier, men do great with a blueprint, and I'm going to give you a blueprint to understand your enemy.

This is what you'll learn in this chapter.

1. How to dispel the "chemical imbalance" myth and learn why depression requires a holistic solution.

2. How trauma impacts your brain and body on a physiological level.

3. Discover the 4 Depression Mechanisms that make up the depression trap.

4. The secret to disarming the depression trap once and for all.

Depression Is a Holistic Problem That Must Be Solved Holistically

There are 3 problems with the way we currently approach depression.

1. Our modern way of dealing with depression isn't holistic.

2. Treating depression as a "chemical imbalance" causes men to resign themselves to an an unfulfilling life and potential suicide.

3. We treat it similarly to how we'd treat a disease instead of an invitation inward.

Let me explain.

Depression impacts your physical, emotional, mental, and even spiritual health (if you're into that type of thing). This is a holistic problem, a whole human problem, and we must have a holistic solution. By now, you probably get that I'm not into the whole "take a pill and cure depression" thing. If a pill helps, then keep taking it, but realize that it's not a cure. There are countless people who take these pills for years and years of their lives but still live a mediocre, or even worse, totally unfulfilled existence. There are some who are so far down that rabbit hole that they're afraid to admit, "The pills aren't working." To admit that would force them to deal with the hard, raw, scary truth of their own pain. Not only that but the hard truth is that we haven't been taught the tools to use for coping with pain. One of the reasons that the pill thing really doesn't work is because physiology is not the whole story.

When men deal with depression, we go get a pill and maybe go see a therapist. Maybe both, but often not either! It's even more rare to get a therapist, a gym membership, a new diet, or some supplements and to explore your own experience of life, including social conditioning, trauma, and family history. This is a massive problem because so many of us suffer, but no one really addresses depression holistically.

And, that is the way to overcome it!

It's scary what we've achieved as a society, all the amenities, all the technology, all the comforts, yet we're more depressed than we've ever been. "What the heck is going on?" you ask. We've conquered the external, but happiness, peace, and contentment comes from knowing yourself. We've completely lost touch, and my methodology is designed to get you in touch and make you truly happy.

The "Chemical Imbalance" Myth

Remember I told you the story about my nurse who told me, "We don't actually know how SSRIs work. We just have to keep trying different dosages." Initially, I thought, "Well, this person must be incompetent, someone must know!" But over years and after doing some reading on the topic, I don't think anyone knows the truth for certain.

If you're unfamiliar with the chemical imbalance theory, the general consensus for a long time was that depression is caused by a lack of serotonin in the brain. They created selective serotonin reuptake inhibitor pills (SSRIs) to block the reabsorption (reuptake) of serotonin into neurons. This makes more serotonin more available to improve transmission of messages between neurons, which would in turn make the depressed person not depressed. It's a simple solution that sounds like it will offer relief, right? Not only was this the exact opposite of my experience and countless others, but it's a hotly debated topic even amongst mental health professionals.

Dr. Joanna Moncrieff, a practicing psychiatrist and professor at University College of London, who writes on the misuse and misrepresentation of psychiatric drugs wrote an article titled *The Chemical Imbalance Theory of Depression: Still*

Promoted but Still Unfounded, where she details the controversy of the chemical imbalance theory of depression. It's based on her and co-author Dr. Mark Horowitz's umbrella review on all the studies that gave birth of using SSRI's in treating depression.

Here's the quick and dirty version.

1. The two brain chemicals that have been said to cause depression are noradrenaline and serotonin (the "feel good" chemical).

2. The evidence on noradrenaline has now been agreed on by the mainstream that lowered or imbalanced levels do NOT contribute to depression.

3. Evidence on serotonin comes from studies on serotonin receptors and serotonin depletion studies.

4. Various serotonin receptor studies have all offered contradictory evidence. Some found lowered levels of serotonin in people with depression compared to those without while others found no difference. Some even found higher levels related to depression. Time and time again, there was nothing that proved that low serotonin contributed to depression.

5. Back in the 1960s and 1970s, they did serotonin depletion studies with a powerful serotonin depleting

chemical called para-chlorophenylalanine. It produced states of insomnia, aggression, hypersexual behavior, irritability, hypersensitivity, agitation, and paranoia but NOTHING resembling depression.

N-O-T-H-I-N-G.

Dr. Moncrieff acknowledges that, obviously, there are brain events and biochemical reactions when someone feels depressed, but there isn't any research that shows a correlation between certain events or reactions and depression.

It's deeply concerning when all of this starts to sink in.

This suggests that our whole perspective of what depression is and how to approach it is built on inconclusive science. This leaves regular guys like us with the completely wrong mindset when approaching depression! Why would we even think that the way we are taught to deal with emotions would have an impact on our mental health? Why would we assume that getting our diet and exercise regimen together would have an impact on an innate "chemical imbalance?" Why would we look back to the past and even be curious about what may have been traumatic? Why would we try to learn how to express our feelings or build a support system?

Do I believe that medication can help? Maybe. There are people that I know that swear by it and have great results. I cannot deny that experience. But what is infuriating to me is the millions of people taking medications to help solve their suffering who never find relief.

Why isn't it working?

Could it be that SSRIs are designed to increase levels of serotonin in the brain when that's not even the problem?

To me, depression is not always a chemical imbalance, and it's not to be treated as a disease. Depression is pain suppressed. It's a lack of space to process the trauma and emotions of life. It's a lack of life-affirming health practices, like a good diet, regular exercise, being outside, and enjoying community. For us men, it's all the ways we've been hamstrung by the image of who we need to be, how we need to act, and the list of everything we're not allowed to express.

Dr. Moncrieff states, "The disease-model, however, is ultimately not helpful, as well as being unfounded. It conveys the message that we are powerless to change ourselves or our situations. When things go wrong, it persuades us we need a pill to put them [the patient] right. This approach may appeal to some people, and I am in no way disparaging those who choose to follow it, but it is important that everyone knows how little evidence there is to support it."

That's something to really look at...

"It conveys the message that we are powerless to change ourselves or our situations."

Right?

We've been taught to believe the idea that depression is just a chemical imbalance and that there's something missing that can only be replaced by a pill. This idea quashes any mental attempt to even think just for a second, "I am going find out what depression is and learn how to cure it."

This begs the question, "If not a chemical imbalance, then what is depression?"

The Secret to Understanding Depression

Ever so often, while writing this book, this question gnaws at me, "Who am I to do this?" I'm explaining a problem that is so complicated that tens of thousands (probably more) of scientists, doctors, mental health professionals, and authors have dedicated their lives to understanding it. Afterall, I'm no PhD, I'm no researcher, and I don't have a long list of patients or clients. The answer to my question always comes back to me, "You were in the belly of the beast."

This is a good lesson for you and me both.

See, we're taught to give ourselves over to the authorities when it comes to most aspects of our health. We often discount personal experiences because of the idea that one person's experience doesn't mean that it's applicable to everyone's experience. That's true, but logic is fast and science is slow. If we don't take the available information (science), evaluate it for ourselves, and combine it with our personal experiences to create some kind of self-authority, we'll just be waiting around for someone else to tell us what to do.

As you know from the last section, that thing might be completely wrong! The process of this chapter, understanding depression, is more than just understanding a problem. You're embarking on a journey of self-discovery that leads to wisdom, self-knowledge, and confidence. You'll get a lot more personal agency to make decisions for yourself because you'll know yourself.

Understanding depression is a process of understanding yourself, and it requires self-reflection, evaluating the world around you, and drawing actionable conclusions (and being open to being wrong).

In Zen Buddhism, there's a concept called *beginner mind*. It's something my sifu would talk about in how to approach learning martial arts and living a happy life. The idea is that you detach from everything you think you know. You play like you don't know anything, like you're a beginner. In this state, your mind is open and you're seeking to understand. This is a different approach than what is typical, which is to come into something holding onto all of our preconceived notions and all the knowledge we've learned. In that state, we close ourselves off to new insights that could be profoundly transformational.

I want you to do the same as you read through this section—be open and seek to understand for yourself. Truthfully, I don't want you to stop there. I want you to get your hands on every book about depression and trauma and fill your mind with thousands of ideas and then discern the truth for yourself.

Alright, to gain an understanding of depression, let's dig into this by starting to look at the definition of depression from the National Institute of Health's website. They have many ways of describing the effects of depression:

- Persistent sad, anxious, or "empty" mood.
- Feelings of hopelessness or pessimism.
- Feelings of irritability, frustration, or restlessness.
- Feelings of guilt, worthlessness, or helplessness.
- Loss of interest or pleasure in hobbies and activities.
- Decreased energy, fatigue, or feeling slowed down.
- Difficulty concentrating, remembering, or making decisions.
- Difficulty sleeping, waking early in the morning, or oversleeping.
- Changes in appetite or unplanned weight changes.

- Physical aches or pains, headaches, cramps, or digestive problems that do not have a clear physical cause and do not go away with treatment.
- Thoughts of death or suicide or suicide attempts.

Does this sound like a collection of all the worst emotions and physical symptoms? How do you go about deciphering that? It almost seems like each set of those symptoms could have its own cause. It kind of makes sense that they stuck with the chemical imbalance theory—it's simple.

We're not going to stop there. We're going to dig for the truth. Like we discussed in the last section, depression is a holistic problem that requires a holistic solution. To understand that problem, we have to get to the root of it. I alluded to this in Chapter 5 when I told the story about the woman with her hand on the hot pan and the doctor that prescribes pain killers. Remember that? Well, we're not going to manage symptoms by numbing the pain. We're going to go to seek to understand the root of the pain and learn to be with it to dissolve it.

In this next section, I'm going to break apart depression into its various pieces and causes. Right now, we mostly view depression as this amorphous blob of horrible, life-threatening feelings, so we're going to pick and pull it apart until you have a new view and understand the following:

1. How trauma and pain turn into depression.

2. The difference between the terms depression and apathy.

3. Why apathy took you over in the first place.

4. The extra layer of confusion that is added by social stigma.

As we start to demystify depression, you'll feel a sense of relief, but there will always be more introspective and understanding work to do as you go on your journey.

How Trauma Turns into Depression

I'm going to give you a short breakdown on how trauma can lead to depression. Then, we'll do a deep inspection of the main mechanisms. You can use the image below as a visual understanding of this flow of events.

The Depression Trap

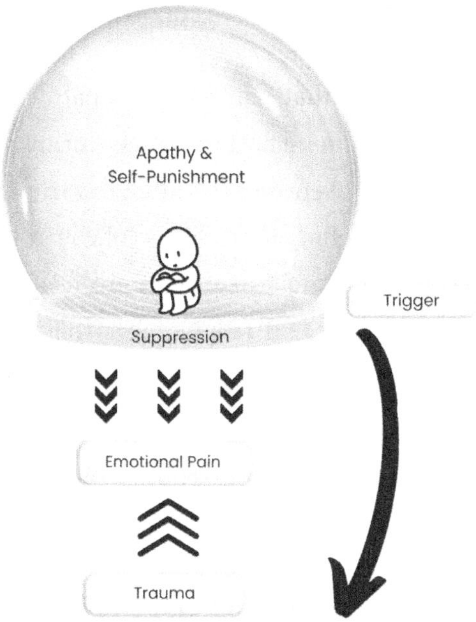
Apathy &
Self-Punishment
Trigger
Suppression
Emotional Pain
Trauma

I've said a few times throughout this book that depression is pain suppressed.

What does that really mean?

Your traumatic experience lives at the core of depression. It's a violation, a victimization, a single incident or ongoing experience, or even social conditioning that hurt you so deeply that, at the time, your brain and body could not process it. It left a wound that causes ongoing pain.

Since we do not have the skills or support to deal with pain and were so indoctrinated with the idea of having to "man-up, shut up, and move on"—we suppress it.

The suppression of that pain creates apathy and self-punishing thoughts, which can take place during, immediately after, or weeks or even months after the traumatic experience. Apathy is a feeling of a total loss of control and inability to take action. It's almost like we've given up on ourselves. It's the hopelessness and helplessness that's so prevalent. Self-punishing thoughts are the abusive thoughts that tell you that you're weak, broken, bad, and they can easily turn into suicidal thoughts, physical self-harm, or suicide.

Depression is that deadly combination of apathy, self-punishing thoughts, unresolved pain from trauma, and the added social stigma of a society that doesn't allow men to feel.

Now you're stuck with three separate but interwoven sets of emotions to cope with. Each requires a different set of tools to cope with and transform them from darkness to light. In *The Courage Method*, we build courage to help you overcome those feelings of apathy so that you can seek support, change your diet, build a regular exercise habit, and do anything that is required to get back down from the pain you experienced during your trauma. Then, you'll learn how to stop suppressing pain and how to heal it through surrender. Courage fights apathy, and surrender heals pain. Then, the whole depression trap falls apart.

Okay, say it with me!

My depression is a combination of apathy, self-punishing thoughts, and pain from trauma. My apathy and self-punishment comes from suppressing the pain of trauma. Building courage will help me fight through apathy, and by stopping suppression, I can heal my pain through surrender.

I need to stress the importance of what you just learned. Reread it 100 times over because this understanding, although simple, provides the blueprint of how you got here in the first place.

To overcome depression, you need to know how trauma brought you to depression and how the method you're learning addresses it.

CHAPTE 7.3:

Compassionate Introspection

We're going to uncover the depression trap more deeply in the next chapter, but learning these inner workings is going to poke and prod at your own experience with trauma and depression. Compassionate introspection is a technique for deepening your understanding of yourself and healing the pain from trauma.

It requires tremendous courage to go into the dark places in life—it's challenging work. You're not going to want to spend months and years of your life doing it. You're going to want to focus on your career, relationships, family, passions—and all of the external things. Doing this internal work is going to make all of those external things possible and so much better.

It is not a normal thing to do to look within. The majority of people will never do it in their lifetime. They will live their lives as a reaction to the circumstances before them, never once looking in and wondering "Why?"

For those of us who have endured trauma and have been stuck with depression, anxiety, or the like, we have no choice. We'd risk living unconsciously, which would lead to an unfulfilling life or even taking our own lives. Without introspection and without intervention, I think you and I both know what the future will look like.

That may sound scary but it is also a relief to know that to interrupt that almost certain future, you just need to look within yourself.

The *Tao Te Ching*, the primary book of Taoist philosophy which has guided my martial arts practice and my life, says, "Knowing the world is wisdom, and knowing yourself is enlightenment."

Enlightenment is idealized as this state of unshakeable happiness, bliss, peace, and contentment. Whether that is a possibility or not, I don't know, but the Tao suggests that by understanding ourselves in mind, body, and spirit, we can achieve something in the direction of enlightenment. There is peace and happiness in knowing, and knowing comes from introspection.

Introspection is looking inward with curiosity and questioning. When we start to ask questions, when it comes to how we feel, why we react the way we do, how we ended up here, and what happened in the past, it opens the doors to knowing ourselves. The process of introspection isn't linear, but I put together a loose framework to get you started on this journey. The more you do it, the more it will become second nature and your process will be unique to you.

1. Get Curious

Your past experiences heavily influence what you believe and how you think and feel in the present. Clearly, you're not loving everything about your present experience, and you're starting to understand that maybe your depression isn't just a chemical imbalance. It's not just a problem born out of trauma and the suppression of that pain but also a lack of self-awareness. As a society, we don't value that deeper, internal understanding of why we are the way we are and essentially asking the question, "What does it mean to be human?" Now, for overcoming depression, we may not have to go that deep, but it's the idea of getting curious that you need to spark within yourself. That curiosity and seeking to understand is at the core of being introspective.

How do you spark genuine curiosity?

By understanding and believing it is your way out. You've briefly seen how the depression trap works and the impact trauma has on your brain and body. This isn't a problem that you can just hand over to the doctor because all the ways out are locked in your brain and body. Yes, you can get the support of a therapist, friends, and family, but this is your journey and you have all the answers inside. You just have to find them. Let the prospect of overcoming this depression fuel the fire of curiousity. On the other side of this internal work is authentic happiness—really and truly.

2. Question Everything

Nothing is off limits—everything must be questioned and dissected. Put on your investigator hat and get out your magnifying glass because it's time to start seeing what's really going on with you. Start by looking at your feelings, thoughts, beliefs, and triggers. Ask yourself, "Where does that come from? Why is it coming up now? Why do I feel this way?" Allow your mind to search. Let it go down the rabbit hole and find the moments in your past that led you to think, feel, and believe the way you do now.

When you don't know the why behind who you are in life, then every part of life becomes harder to navigate. If you don't understand your reactions, then you suppress them. When there's a challenge on your path that makes you anxious or uncomfortable, you quit instead of facing the feeling head on. It's almost like all the ways you've been conditioned (through experiences, trauma, society, and media) set you on an almost certain future path. Without questioning yourself and challenging yourself, you're stuck on that path.

Questioning can take place in many forms. You can start to journal a few times a week and just let your thoughts out onto the page. Let them flow. Write everything you've been holding in. Give your brain the space to process something external but privately. You can just go on long walks and listen to music. Notice what comes into your mind and follow it. You can find practices that act like catalysts for that change, that force you to rethink your thoughts, feelings, and beliefs. Of course, there's therapy, which is a crucial part of my methodology, but there are more avenues you can add. It could be meditation, yoga, breathing exercises, or classes. It could be a men's group where you can explore, share, and feel understood for what you're going through. It could be weeklong retreats, weekend seminars, or heck, saving up a bunch of money and traveling to another country.

It could be anything to get you to challenge your preconceived notions about yourself and your life. The key here is to start to connect your past to your present. You want to see how life made you the way you are. This awareness alone will help you begin to unwind the things about your thoughts, feelings, and beliefs that are getting in your way or making you miserable. Inevitably, as you start to understand how you came to these conclusions, you're going to have some feelings come up.

3. Feel Everything

Nothing is off limits. Start to shut down the automatic emotion suppression system and feel whatever comes up in the process of questioning. Identify the feelings that arise. Do they make you feel sad? Angry? Happy? Forlorn? Confused? Stressed? Be present and focus on identifying those feelings. Say them aloud if necessary. You may also notice that you have feelings about your feelings. You may feel sad and another a part of you will be mad that you're sad. You may feel angry but then guilt or shame about feeling angry. This is normal. Don't judge it. Just identify your feelings. Emotions are complicated, and I've heard them explained as wild horses. They gallop through the great plain with their own rhyme and their own rhythm. Sometimes, what arises won't make complete sense or have a definitive reason—just learn to be with your feelings and follow where they lead. They may bring you to a place that you don't want to be but desperately need to be to overcome this depression. They will lead you through the darkness and out into the light. They are a part of this human experience, and the more time you spend with them, the less overwhelming they will feel. They are parts of yourself. Rejecting your emotions is like rejecting yourself, which is exactly what we're trying to undo.

4. Be Compassionate

This process isn't about harsh self-judgment and self-punishment. Your mind, at times, will attempt to go down that path, but gently redirect it. Redirect it to a place of love and care for yourself. The reason you're here is because you're in pain, and we haven't been taught what to do with pain to heal it. It starts with offering yourself the care that you may never have been taught or never received. When is the last time you told yourself, "I'm going to make it. It's okay that you feel this way. I'm here for you. I love you."? Just saying words of love and encouragement to yourself can be a transformational experience. You've got to figure that right now, your brain is wired for all the terrible thoughts you think about yourself and life. I'm sure you've got a few phrases that run through your head over and over again. Those pathways are like superhighways in your brain. You probably think those thoughts without consciously trying to think them. They probably happen so quickly that you get the sense that it's another voice in your head that isn't yours. To be honest, it's scary.

In this process of introspection, you need to add compassion. As you dive into the past, following your emotions and questioning every little thing, add in self-love. Give yourself those kind and caring words. It doesn't sound badass, and it doesn't sound tough. You're probably feeling some level of resistance at the thought of even doing it! This is the exact reason you need to start doing it. Imagine if those superhighways of negative self-talk transformed into superhighways of positive self-talk. What if you became your biggest cheerleader? What if, when you were down and out, you had a voice that lifted you up? What if there was someone who was always there for you and that person was you? It's something you have to build within yourself.

Notes on Internal Exploration

Note 1: The clues to your past are in your present.

The thing about suppression is that you're not just pushing away feelings but you're suppressing the memories of pain that create those feelings. Often, I found it hard to understand why I felt the way I felt because the suppression was so strong. It's kind of like the eruption of Mount Vesuvius, spewing volcanic ash all over Pompeii, burying the entire city for thousands of years. You have to be like an archaeologist and use the clues that come up now to uncover your forgotten city of memories. When you get triggered by something—that is a clue. When you get upset or hurt unexpectedly—that is a clue. When you have a strong thought about a certain topic—that is a clue. These clues show up throughout your daily life. You just need to start paying more attention. The reason that we miss them is because they feel uncomfortable, and we either suppress them or deny them without a second thought. They are so close to us and who we are that it's hard to distinguish that it may have come from trauma we experienced.

Note 2: Study yourself under one thousand lights.

There's a saying in kung fu to "study your kung fu under one thousand lights." It means that you shouldn't *just* do the forms, drills, and practice as you are told. You have a unique body and a unique mind. The style is a methodology for learning how to fight. You have to actively participate in understanding how it applies to you. The same goes for you. Unfortunately, this process isn't going to be linear. If anything, it's going to be circular and maybe even a little chaotic. So, you need to be an active participant in unwinding your depression and healing your trauma. You need to look at it from different angles, revisit different conditions, explore deeper, step away, rest, and return.

Note 3: Don't get caught in intellectualization.

We talked about this earlier in this book, but it's definitely worth a reminder. As you're going through this process, don't get stuck in the trap of intellectualization. I spent many years thinking that I was "doing the work" because I could map out the entire web of my life, but I was missing the emotional component. This process can easily turn into an intellectual game, but it won't help you process the pain, which is the key to dissolving your depression.

CHAPTER 7.4:

The Depression Trap

There are four mechanisms that make up the depression trap. By identifying and understanding each mechanism, you will gain a better understanding of how to overcome depression. Like I said, understanding the problem is the key to creating an effective solution. It's impossible to learn about the depression trap without thinking about your own experiences. If you need to step away, time to think, or time to process things, then do it. Call a friend, take a walk, go to the gym, or cook dinner. Sometimes, we need to let our brains work out understandings for us.

You might experience wanting to figure it all out and fix it all as you're learning, which can be stressful, overwhelming, and lead to negative self-talk. Remember what I said at the outset of this journey: "Just read the book." You may not know it but by reading, you're starting to unravel depression. Your brain is starting to categorize and understand the problem you're facing. By the end of this chapter, you're really going to have a handle on what's ailing you and what you'll need to do to disarm it. Then, in the following chapters, I'm going to give you the techniques you need to dismantle the depression trap. By the end of this book, in Chapter 9, I'm going to give you the four-step process for implementing the whole methodology. So, if it all feels like an amorphous blob of knowledge, insights, and techniques...GOOD! That's where you should be!

Nothing needs to be fixed right now. Just keep reading this book.

Depression Mechanism #1: The Trauma

The first depression mechanism lies at the root of your depression: trauma. In this section, you'll get a deeper understanding of the impact that trauma has on your brain and body. There's a plethora of information you can find on the topic of trauma, and I encourage that you read more beyond this book. I'm going to provide you with what you absolutely need to know, but if you need more, head over to the resources section at the end of this book for some suggestions.

Trauma results from an experience of extreme stress or pain that leaves an individual feeling helpless or too overwhelmed to cope with adversity. Experiences involving war, violent crimes, or rape but also mental and emotional abuse (especially at a young age) can cause trauma to the brain and body. These experiences can be a single incident, an ongoing repetitive experience, or a complex web of both.

You may have come to this book just looking for the solution to depression and might not have an obvious experience of trauma, like war, physical violence, or sexual abuse. Don't let social stigmas around trauma prevent you from identifying experiences that caused trauma. Because of the "man up, shut up, and move on" way of how we're taught to navigate the world as men, you may have buried something that was severely traumatic. Acknowledging trauma can be challenging and even unbelievable at times.

If you feel like you're straying too deep, then take a break. A lot of this work requires the help of a therapist along with using your best judgment. Delving into your past can be upsetting and triggering, which can leave you in a deeper depressive state for days or weeks. Without the right tools and support, it can be almost impossible to navigate. Go slow and don't poke at anything that you don't think you can handle alone.

Trauma's Effect on the Brain

We've learned a lot about the brain, but there are still many mysteries left that leave gaps in our collective understanding about brain function. What we do understand is that trauma has profound and lasting effects on the brain and can alter its structure.

3 Areas that are Affected

1. **Neural Pathways:** Information and communication highways of the brain.

2. **The Amygdala:** Responsible for processing emotions and triggering the body's stress response.

3. **The Hippocampus:** Crucial in memory formation and emotional regulation.

In a traumatic incident, whether it was singular or ongoing abuse, the amygdala triggers the body's stress response, or fight-or-flight, which elevates the body's cortisol levels and sometimes even releases adrenaline. During a fight-or-flight response, your body tries to prioritize, so anything it doesn't need for immediate survival is placed on the back burner. This means that digestion, reproductive and growth hormone production, and tissue repair are all temporarily halted. A fight-or-flight response increases the heart rate and blood glucose levels preparing the body to act. For people who have experienced trauma, the brain can remain in a stress response, causing elevated chronic cortisol levels.

Over time, these high cortisol levels can reduce the size of the hippocampus and impair its function, leading to difficulties with memory, learning, and emotional regulation. If you've ever noticed that your emotional states are hard to manage or that you have gaps in memory, this could be the reason.

Additionally, these chronically high cortisol levels can inhibit neuroplasticity (the brain's ability to form new pathways based on new experiences), making it more difficult for the brain to adapt and change in response to new information or experiences. This means that after the trauma is over, the brain's ability to rewire itself to the new experience is inhibited. This is one of the reasons why many trauma survivors go on to have persistent chronically high cortisol levels. The old "wiring" from the traumatized brain hasn't been rewired, so the brain takes in new experiences but can misidentify them as threats like the trauma.

This misidentification causes the amygdala to trigger the stress response again, and again, and again. Without intervention, this process can go on indefinitely and causes serious harm not just to the person's well-being but also to the immune and endocrine system, dumping more cortisol and continuing the cycle. Not only that but the high cortisol levels can enhance the reactivity of the amygdala. This is why people with trauma can so easily find themselves in a stressed out state over the "smallest" incidents or obstacles.

If this all sounds like a bunch of scientific jargon, let's talk about an actual experience. I'll give you some more details in the upcoming section on apathy and self-punishing thoughts. For a period in my life, I was stuck in a mentally and emotionally abusive relationship. The constant manipulation, gaslighting, blame shifting, criticism, belittling, and moodswings changed my brain. Not only had I descended into cynicism and apathy on an emotional level but my whole experience of life was dominated by this stress response.

Everyday, I was overwhelmed, worried, scared, and on edge. My amygdala was being triggered by the threat of being yelled at, shamed, blamed, or guilted. Cortisol flooded my system all day, every day. After I got out of the situation and went to college, that stress response didn't stop. Since the chronically high cortisol levels had shrunk my hippocampus and inhibited my brain's neuroplasticity, I was unable to cope with my emotional states, and my brain couldn't rearrange itself to the new environment I was in. It began to react to new stimuli in the same old way. A professor's disapproving look in my direction activated a deep fear. A paper due in three weeks caused unproportionate amounts of stress. Going to sleep at night was impossible because I was locked in that high state of stress. Even though I had left the situation, not only was the damage already done but the damage was ongoing.

If the sound of this causes you worry, I totally get it. When I learned this, I felt like I was trapped and my brain was seriously broken, but don't worry. You're not broken. This is all fixable, and by following my method, you'll start to undo what was done. Remember, you don't have to *do* anything just yet. Just keep reading this book.

Trauma's Effect on the Body

The impact trauma has on the brain has a domino effect resulting in the body changing too. The high cortisol levels and adrenaline spikes from that repetitive stress response can have devastating effects on different systems of the body. One of the systems is called the autonomic nervous system which controls heart rate, blood pressure, respiration, and digestion. There are two branches of the autonomic nervous system: the sympathetic and the parasympathetic. (If you're having flashbacks of high school biology, I get it, this one always tripped me up!) The sympathetic system controls all of the fight-or-flight functions and the parasympathetic controls all of the rest-and-digest functions.

Now, imagine with me for a moment. If your body is caught in that constant cycle of stress response and your body lives amidst the functions of the sympathetic system, what would happen?

You would experience a regularly increased heart rate, inhibited digestive function, difficulties with tissue repair, and high levels of emotional stress. You can only imagine the effect this could have over multiple years. Not only would your body live in this state but your body would be barred from important parasympathetic functions, like a slow heartbeat, proper digestive function, the ability to repair tissue, and low stress levels.

All this prolonged exposure to stress hormones can weaken the immune system, disrupt sleep patterns, induce chronic pain, and cause headaches, stomach issues, and cardiovascular problems. Remember when we looked at the NIH definition of depression and it had all of those physical symptoms? I hope it's all becoming a bit less mysterious to you.

Another way trauma affects the physical body is how trauma can be stored in the body's musculature and tissues through patterns of tension and tightness.

Now, I know this might sound a little more 'woo-woo,' but I promise this is a real phenomenon that's called body armoring. Body armoring is an idea that originated in the field of somatic psychology pioneered by Wilhelm Reich. It holds that unconscious muscular tensions and patterns are created in traumatic experiences that put us into that fight-or-flight mode. These tensions are believed to create a physical "armor" that shields us from unresolved traumas, stress, and negative emotions. Although this is the body's attempt to protect us, it is another way of holding or suppressing the pain of trauma. Many people have used various bodywork techniques, like myofascial release, craniosacral therapy, and massage therapy, with the intent to release this tension and the pain of trauma that lies beneath the surface.

In my first life career as a massage therapist, I often experienced this with clients who would burst into tears during or after sessions. As a culture, we're very disconnected from how interconnected our minds, bodies, and emotions truly are. My path as a massage therapist and as a martial artist has brought about a deep understanding of all of these connections that are often overlooked by western modalities of healing.

You probably see why when I talk about trauma and depression, I say it's a holistic problem. It's a whole human problem that affects everything: body, mind, and spirit. When you start to uncover what's actually going on and look back at the chemical imbalance theory, it's quite frustrating.

This whole methodology is built to be a holistic solution to this holistic problem we call depression. After you finish this chapter, I'll start to provide the various techniques to get you out of the depression trap. Next stop—understanding suppression.

Compassionate Introspection Exercise

Grab a notebook and write down what you're thinking and feeling. Try and answer the questions below. If any emotions arise, simply breathe and be with them.

1. Can you identify 3 situations that you react differently to after your traumatic incident? Does it feel like you're in control?

2. How often do you feel stressed, on edge, or worried throughout the day?

If nothing comes to the surface, then let it be and keep reading. But, if at any point an insight arises, take a moment, start practicing feeling these things, and let them flow through you without resistance.

Depression Mechanism #2: Suppression

There are only a few ways we're taught to deal with emotions, not just as men but as a culture. As men, there's an additional layer of pressure to not be emotional—"man up, shut up, and move on." But, we are just human, and part of being human is having emotional experiences—they are an inevitability. Not only that but emotions are part of how our bodies function and process our experiences.

For a lot of guys, feeling and expressing emotions has been deemed a sign of weakness. It is not a sign of weakness but a simple fact of life. With that, we need to figure out what to do with our emotions, particularly the painful ones.

Like I mentioned earlier, feelings of apathy are the result of pain being suppressed. If we were taught or "allowed" to feel and process that pain, we would avoid all of the apathy, the depression, and the ongoing suffering. The most frightening and exciting truth is that sometimes it only takes a moment to be able to let go of a painful emotion to transform your life, but it requires courage to go there and sit in the fire so to speak.

In this section, we're going to break down the mechanism of suppression. You'll learn a couple things:

- The difference between repression and suppression.

- How the suppression mechanism is a core piece of the depression cycle (without it, the whole system cannot function).

The Difference Between Repression and Suppression

Up until now, I have not made a distinction between suppression and repression, but it's important to know that there is a difference. Suppression and repression are two different ways of pushing pain and emotions out of the present moment. Repression is considered to be an unconscious act, whereas suppression is a conscious act.

Repression

Repression is a defense mechanism that pushes distressing thoughts, feelings, and memories out of conscious awareness. It is an unconscious defense mechanism to protect you from experiences that may be too overwhelming to deal with—like trauma. Since repression operates unconsciously, you may not be aware that you are engaging in it, and it's very hard to actually control. Through therapy, you can work to exhume and process those repressed experiences, which is going to be tremendously helpful in undoing your apathy.

Suppression

On the other hand, suppression is the conscious act of pushing distressing thoughts, feelings, and memories out of conscious awareness. This is like when someone bothers you or something reminds you of a stressful event. You notice the thoughts and feelings and consciously say, "I don't want to deal with that," and push it away.

A friend once described it to me this way, "Whenever I have a bad feeling, I put it in a little bottle, cap it, swallow it, and it disappears in my stomach."

That's suppression.

Men are more wired by society for suppression. We don't even have to think about it because we're not really "allowed" to have or express emotions. From a young age, we built this automatic system to stamp out any sign of emotions, especially ones that have been characterized as more feminine emotions or experiences. You know the drill; you can be happy and you can be angry—everything else... That's for girls.

This cuts out hundreds of human experiences from our lives and leads to higher rates of depression and suicide. We cannot even talk about it because it errs on the side of "too emotional" and might be perceived as weakness.

It's a horrible trap, and the way out is simple but against our conditioning: stop suppressing feelings.

It's not that easy.

I have been calling it the automatic emotion suppression system for a reason. Although, it's not completely unconscious like repression, which you would never even notice when it occurs. This automatic emotion suppression system has very quick reflexes when it comes to emotions that haven't been deemed manly by society. Just by starting to pay attention and acknowledge how often this system activates, you are doing the work to disarm it.

Suppression also comes from not knowing what to do with emotions. Some experiences may nudge an emotional reaction out of you. You acknowledge them in the moment, don't enjoy how they feel. Because you don't really know what to do with them, you push them away.

These systems of not dealing with pain results in the build up of these unprocessed emotions, which leads to apathy. Apathy and self-punishing thoughts are an indicator that you're overloaded with unresolved pain. You've surpassed your quota, you've crossed the limit, and there's no more space to hold your pain.

Part of being human is having and expressing emotions, and when we cut off that entire part of our experience, we start to shut down, give up, go numb, and develop a self-hating voice.

I want you to imagine for a moment that you had a way to call up repressed experiences and resolve that pain, that you knew what to do with your feelings and emotions and were able to deal with them head on, and that after your trauma you had these skills and support at your disposal or gained them somewhere earlier in your journey with depression.

Where would you be now if you had healed that pain?

Without suppressing your emotions and healing that pain, your life would look very different because this whole trap of depression wouldn't have been born. Learning to identify emotions, knowing what to do with them, and learning how to heal pain will unlock the depression trap. This is why I dedicated an entire section of this book to this called the Art of Alchemy. We'll get to that, but for now, there's still more for you to understand about the depression trap. Apathy is next.

Compassionate Introspection Exercise

Grab a notebook and write down what you're thinking and feeling. Try and answer a few of the questions below. For any emotions that arise, simply breathe and be with them.

1. What happens when you feel an emotion?

2. What do you say to yourself when you're feeling an emotion?

3. What would happen if you let that emotion be there?

4. Who or what told you that it wasn't okay to feel or express your emotions? When did it happen?

If nothing comes to the surface, then let it be and keep reading. If at any point an insight arises, take a moment, start practicing feeling these things, and let them flow through you without resistance.

Depression Mechanism #3: Apathy and Self-Punishment

Apathy is the result of the suppression of pain from trauma. It is the feeling that is most characteristic of depression. Apathy is the belief of "I can't." It's this deep sense that you can't do anything about your life situation like you've lost agency over your life. Not only that but it's the pervasive feeling that no one can help you. It's a deep state of not caring, discouragement, defeat, isolation, withdrawal, depletion, pessimism, meaninglessness, helplessness, failure, despair, confusion, doom, and gloom. Eventually, there is a point where apathy applies to every aspect of life, including the prospect of getting out of depression.

Since we're not prescribing you a pain pill for a burning hand and we want to get to the root of the problem, we must return back to where apathy set in. The best way I can do this is by sharing my experience, but I want you to search for yourself. Look into your past and see if there is a similar moment. By identifying the moment where you gave up, you can gain a lot of insight into the pervasive behaviors of your present and get a deeper understanding of your triggers.

For those who have experienced trauma, there's a moment when what we have endured was too much for our brains. It was too confusing, conflicting, horrifying, painful, scary, or overwhelming, and we gave in. It's the moment when we gave up our will and began our descent into apathy, anxiety, dissociation, etc. and we solidified our way of being a victim.

Whether it was caused by extreme emotional stress, physical violence, sexual assault, or devastating mental and emotional manipulation, we can look back and say, "That was the moment where I broke."

I believe it's often why people with trauma or depression will say that they are broken or unfixable—it's because of this moment.

I won't bore you with all of my personal details, but essentially, I was in an emotionally and mentally abusive relationship for many years. I could never do anything right, I was constantly put down or ignored when I spoke, and there were myriad other things that drained my confidence. I can remember the moment where I completely broke with crystal clarity. That moment wasn't out of the ordinary in any way.

I was already dissociating because it was the only way I learned to deal with his angry rants and unpredictable behavior. He would go on and on, and I decided in my mind that I gave up. He could have it all. He wanted me to feel so badly about myself. He didn't want to hear or listen to me speak. Everything I did was so wrong and deficient. Then, he would get the person he created. I gave into the darkness of the world he had created around us. I broke. I gave up my will to live. I didn't have a way of dealing with the pain and I couldn't see a path out of the situation.

I chose apathy.

I used to hold a lot of shame around everything that happened. Why did I stay? How could his "bad mood" affect me so much? Why was I so weak? Looking back, it all makes sense. I let go of the shame I had around being traumatized because I realized that shame is a part of being victimized. It was the same mechanism that was installed in my brain by the trauma. It was NOT something I did wrong but something wrong that was done to me. I refused to blame myself, I refused to hide what happened to me, and I didn't want to lose even more time in *my* life.

I share this to illustrate the moment when I broke and descended into total apathy. If you haven't already, can you identify a similar moment when you chose apathy over life, when what you were enduring was just too much and the light left your eyes? If you've got a lot coming up, then take a moment to write, go for a walk, listen to your favorite music, breathe, or cry.

Self-Punishment and Suicide

It's not only apathy that is created by the suppression of pain. There are also the self-punishing thoughts. It's the self-hatred, the worthlessness, the negativity, and the warped vision of yourself. The pain that is being suppressed doesn't just "disappear in your stomach" like my friend noted. That pain seeps up like sewage through manhole covers and poisons your reality. Self-punishing thoughts are the warped calls for help by parts of yourself that are suffering. These thoughts are perpetuated by the social stigma of being a man with depression. They're oozing with guilt, shame, and blame. They come from a place of not understanding that the trauma and depression is not your fault. They come from a lack of understanding that your reaction to what happened is normal and expected. Along with apathy, these are the two ways of being that so fundamentally characterize the experience of depression.

Apathy and self-punishment, at the highest level, can easily turn to suicidal thoughts, planning, and then suicide. I cannot tell you how many times I wished myself to be dead or how many times I had the thought of putting a gun in my mouth, the people in my life finding me, and a funeral taking place. I lived with those thoughts of suicide for years, and there are only a select few people in my life that I disclosed that to. Sadly, in our society, it's not something that we can talk about openly, but it's exactly what is needed. If those thoughts and feelings, and ultimately the underlying pain, are not about to be expressed, then action soon follows.

If you're experiencing suicidal thoughts, images in your mind, or plan to do it, please reach out to someone. If the situation is dire, I've included a suicide hotline in the resource section of this book. Also, go to Chapter 11 and use my method for finding a therapist fast. You need an outlet for this pain, and you deserve an opportunity to heal.

I'll continue to beat this drum that the access to dialing the suicide hotline, finding a therapist, or telling your mother, father, sister, brother, or friend that you are considering killing yourself—takes courage. Crossing the boundary of fear, shame, and discomfort to reach out for help is part of this battle. Don't overthink it, but be smart. Reach out to someone that you trust will be supportive because not everyone can handle it. Don't let that stop you from reaching out for help. As you read through this book, you'll build the warrior within you, and as you take action or resist action, you will build courage.

You're going to learn to develop courage systematically in The Warrior's Way in the next chapter, and it will help you dismantle the heavy mood of apathy so you can have more freedom to act. It will allow you to start confronting the pain that you've been suppressing. As you begin to dismantle the automatic emotion suppression system and heal from the pain of your trauma, apathy, and self-punishment, suicidal thoughts will start to fade.

Compassionate Introspection Exercise

Grab a notebook and write down what you're thinking and feeling. Try and answer a few of the questions below. For any emotions that arise, simply breathe and be with them. Don't resist. There's a lot of pain there, so cry it out if necessary. It's okay.

1. Can you identify the moment where you gave in to apathy?

2. Where did the pain that you're holding back come from?

3. How is the trauma you experienced related to your negative self-talk?

4. Are there certain phrases or thoughts that repeat over and over?

If nothing comes to the surface, then let it be and keep reading. If at any point an insight arises, take a little space, start practicing feeling these things, and let them flow through you without resistance.

Depression Mechanism #4: The Trigger

I'm sitting in the passenger seat.

My partner and I are headed out of the city and into the mountains for a weekend camping trip. The car is packed to the brim, and our dogs are happy, panting, drool dripping, and noses turned up to the cracked windows, smelling the first tastes of sweet mountain air.

We'd been planning this trip for months. We secured the best campsite that lives at the end of a small peninsula, jutting out into the lake. We would be surrounded by water, forests, and mountains for a long weekend just to unwind, relax, and soak in nature's vibes.

Soon, we're winding through lush mountainscapes covered with rhododendron, towering oaks, and of course, large vines of poison ivy sneaking through the forests. In the course of our conversations about our last few days of work, plans of buying a home, and more immediate conversations on who was going to set up the tent, we called out clouds that looked like whales, creatures hiding among the bramble, and the occasional waterfalls as we zipped through mountain roads.

Then...my partner said something. He went on a bit of rant. He had too much emotion in his voice. Something. What was it? Not sure. Did I get interrupted? Dismissed? Something...

My mind warped and my vision started to dim. It felt like someone was pushing a cement block against my chest. I became distant and far away like I was watching myself from the peaks of the mountain we once admired. My body got the unexplainable, empty feeling like my soul had left. I felt sad, overwhelmingly sad, and tears wanted to push through my eyes.

My mind thought, "I just don't want to be here."

Over and over.

I saw flashes in my mind of the day I gave in, my abuser ranting, and me staring off, repeating "I don't matter. My life doesn't matter. Who I am doesn't matter. I don't want to be here."

My partner placed his hand on my leg. "Are you there?"

The touch sent fear up my spine, and I looked at him like a scared animal.

"What's happening? Are you okay? Did I do something?" He said.

I stuttered, almost unable to speak, "I... I... I... Here again. I'm gone. I'm sorry."

It wasn't the first time, and it certainly wasn't the last time.

Would this triggered moment turn into a 10-day depressive episode? Was everything that we worked for, the money to secure the site, the time we took off from work, and all the planning, going to be an absolute waste? Was I going to spend days laying on the tent floor, hating myself and the life I worked so hard to build?

Was I going to spend the weekend feeling no sense of joy towards the beauty we'd soon be surrounded by?

Was I going to ruin this trip and eventually my relationship?

My mind was off to the races, and I lost control.

If you've experienced anything like this before, then you've been triggered.

Understanding Triggers

"Whenever you get triggered, somebody pulls that trigger. But who's the one carrying the ammunition, who's the one with the mechanism to deliver the ammunition, who's the one with the explosive material inside them? Where do you want to put your attention? Do you want to put your attention on the trigger purely? Or are you curious about what ammunition or explosive material you're carrying inside? Triggers are really great to work with—if you want to get to know yourself."-Dr. Gabor Mate

There's a lot of talk around the word 'trigger' along with a lot of other terms from the psychological field which has created this pop psychology culture. One pro is that mental health is getting more visibility, but the downside is that terms are often mixed up from their original definitions. The word 'trigger' has become a popular term to describe something that causes any kind of emotional reaction. Some people will even jokingly say, "I'm so triggered right now," with a smile on their face. It does a disservice to the people who do have trauma because when they do get triggered, it's hard to have a smile on your face.

So then, what is a trigger?

Let's look at the analogy itself.

Here are the 3 Parts:

1. Someone or something pulling the trigger.
2. The trigger itself.
3. The ammunition or "explosive material."

First, there's an initiating event that pulls the trigger. It could be a smell, a sound, a touch, a place, or a person, anything that reminds your brain and body of the trauma that you originally experienced. All of a sudden, the pain of that trauma that has been suppressed is opened up. It's like pressing on a raw nerve. The pain and the reaction is uncontrollable, jarring, and usually sets off the body's stress response, flooding the body with stress hormones. It can come out as fear, anger, dissociation, rage, sadness, anxiety, flashbacks, shallow and rapid breathing, and physical or emotional pain. It's similar to when a bullet is fired from a gun. After the trigger is pulled, there's no stopping that bullet now.

Triggers have the power to transport your body and mind through time, taking you from a bright, sunny day in the park to the worst moment or times in your life. Since we're not given the tools to process trauma, we're left with moving on and suppression. But, all of that pain continues to live inside you. It's hiding in the background—loaded. That pain that's locked in the body and mind is really waiting and wants to be healed.

If you flip back to the depression trap image, you'll see that the trigger takes you back to the pain of your trauma. Since we don't have the tools to deal with that pain, just like when the trauma originally happened, we go straight back into the depression trap. Round and round we go, suppressing pain, feeling terrible, with external stimuli triggering that pain sending us deeper and deeper into depression.

As you start to identify your triggers, you'll notice what typically comes after them is a deeper depressive episode. It's important to draw a distinction between depressive episodes and your general depressive mood. Your general depressive mood is the ever present storm cloud above your head that makes your world dark and gloomy. Then, there are these deeper depressive episodes that intensify apathy and self-punishing thoughts. We'll explore what you can do in the wake of these triggers to take care of yourself in Chapter 7.6.

Compassionate Introspection Exercise

Grab a notebook and write down what you're thinking and feeling. Try and answer a few of the questions below. Take a moment to reflect on the last few months.

Your triggers will typically relate back to the moment or situation that caused your trauma. For me, it can be loud noises or yelling that resembles anger. It is being in spaces (specifically the passenger seat of a car) where I don't have freedom to leave and incessant talking without being acknowledged.

Just notice if you're starting to see a pattern. As you go deeper, you'll be able to identify the cues that trigger you and be more present in those times or start to avoid them altogether until you gain more control.

1. Were there times when your depression intensified, and what experience preceded that?

2. Identify 3 sensory experiences or situations that put you in a stressed, highly-emotional, or on-edge state.

3. How are these related to the trauma you experienced?

The Pin That Holds the Trap Together

Hopefully, you are starting to see that the depression trap is a cycle.

At the core of this cycle is one gear that, if we remove it, the whole mechanism, falls apart. It's like taking one pin out of a clock. All of a sudden, it stops ticking. It stops working.

That lynch pin is suppression.

If you stop suppressing pain, then pain can be healed. Without suppressed pain, apathy and self-punishing thoughts disappear and the clouds begin to clear. Without that suppressed pain waiting to be triggered, there is nothing to be triggered. Without all of that, there is no more depression.

You're being equipped with everything that you need to overcome depression. It takes building courage, a willingness to go into the darkness, consistent effort over time, and support. I want to congratulate you on doing this work and getting this far through the book. You have a lot of things working against you right now, and it's clear that you have the dedication it takes to go on this journey. Overcoming depression and living a happy, fulfilled life is possible. Just keep going.

CHAPTER 7.5:

Fighting Depression

"Every action you take is a vote for the type of person you wish to become. No single instance will transform your beliefs, but as the votes build up, so does the evidence of your new identity."

— James Clear

Now that you understand the power of courage and how depression works, you're ready to learn how to build courage with The Warrior's Way. From the outside, The Warrior's Way looks like you're *just* building habits. The Warrior's Way builds structures in your life and your brain that are going to send you in a completely different trajectory. The courage that you develop will give you the mental and emotional fortitude to get through anything. If you just do this, even if you rip this book in half and throw out the second half, it will change your life. But, don't do that! There are more components to overcoming trauma and depression that are in the rest of this book that you'll need too!

Let's start by laying a few ground rules that you can refer to as guides for maintaining balance and ensuring that the process works as intended. Then, I'll give you a few more thoughts on the process itself and end with the five core habits I recommend to get you started.

The 5 Rules of The Warrior's Way:

1. Choose habits that will improve your mental, emotional, and physical health.

2. Start with habits that are going to be low lifts so you can begin developing your courage muscle.

3. Focus on one at a time. Establish the practice into a habit then layer on the next one.

4. Choose practices that challenge YOUR status quo. The practice must always challenge you because without that, there will be nothing to take action against or resist, which is the primary mechanism for developing courage (refer back to Chapter 4 if needed).

5. Keep it chill. It's easy to get overwhelmed, feel weak, and let the depressive mind sabotage this whole process. Slow is smooth, and smooth is fast.

The Impact of Your Habits

We have to understand why it's so important to change your habits by looking at the impact that habits have on your life. Take a look at your life. What are the things that you do day in and day out that operate on autopilot? Is there a certain set of things that you do every morning or every evening? Do you have a coffee as soon as you wake up without fail? Do you watch TV every evening? Do you listen to certain music on the ride to and from work everyday? (Note: this is not an exercise that is judging, blaming, or shaming. This is just to make you more aware of the impact of your habits.)

For me, for a solid decade of my life, the first thing I would do every morning was wake up, start the coffee maker, use the bathroom, pour the coffee, and rush outside to have a cigarette, day in and day out.

What do you think the long-term effect of this habit had on my life?

Not only was I ruining the daily quality of my life but I was contributing towards some future disease or disorder. This habit contributed to a certain direction that my life would go in. Then, if you layered on the myriad other daily, weekly, or monthly habits in my life, you could probably feed it into AI with my genetic profile and my history, and the AI could probably push out a pretty accurate depiction of where I'd end up—if I did not interrupt those habits.

Habits are not just practices that we program ourselves to do without consequence. Habits that we choose, both unconsciously and consciously, determine our future. If we build the habit of exercising three times a week, there's a pretty high chance that you're going to live longer. If you don't, you won't.

It's pretty simple.

I mean, think back to some of those daily or weekly habits you identified. Can you track where they came from, when you started doing them, why you started them, or how long it took for it to take hold as a habit? Most were probably unconscious and a reaction to whatever was going on in your life. Do you want an unconscious reaction to determine your future, or do you want to be in control and be the one that has a say in YOUR future?

What if we chose 3 to 5 practices that we know would improve your mental, emotional, and physical health and, one by one, installed them like programs into your life? What if we took a 90-day period to focus on just one daily practice and worked on being consistent to the point that it could become part of your life? At the start, there's going to be some resistance. There are going to be times when you have to take action when you don't want to or resist taking action when you want to take action.

It's going to activate and develop that part of your brain in the anterior mid-cingulate cortex and grow that muscle to be more easily accessible in the future. Then, after 60 or 90 days of doing that one practice day in and day out, it's going to become easier to do. Eventually, the anterior mid-cingulate cortex is not going to activate as much because that practice will have become so deeply ingrained in your daily routine. The resistance to doing it will mostly disappear. Then, we're going to need to start working on turning another practice to support your mental, emotional, and physical health into a habit.

You see, this process of layering the habits not only develops the anterior midcingulate cortex in your brain but it also starts building these habits as structures in your life which will change the trajectory of your future.

This is a long-term game, and I'm going to show you how to win it.

Your #1 Biggest Obstacle to the Long Game

Rome wasn't built in a day, they told us. Remember hearing that old adage? Well...it's kind of B.S. because we were told one thing but taught another. We live in a world where everything needs to happen now! Even things that are impossible to immediately achieve, like building a house, finding a career we love, working through relationship issues, or starting a business. Now! Getting the perfect score, the right diet, a sexy body, and some cool artistic abilities. Now!

The truth is...everything meaningful and worthwhile takes time. Now...look, I don't have a problem with urgency or a go-get-em attitude towards life. In fact, I firmly believe it's a great way to make things happen in life and the world.

Momentum is powerful.

It's not the attitude that's the problem. It's the hot need for instant gratification. For centuries, advertisers have tantalized the masses with products and services. They've honed the art of making you want and need something newer, better, and in America, bigger. Advertising is a fact of life in the world we've built... Fine. But, the problem is that we're now walking around with handheld advertising devices sneakily disguised as communication devices. We shouldn't have to pay cell phone bills...they should have to pay us for having these deceptive things.

Remember when social media was ad-free? Remember how they slowly snuck adverts in between posts. Now, the average person sees over 2 million ads per year... That's right. TWO MILLION! Two millions ads specifically targeted towards their likes, dislikes, behaviors, and demographics not to mention algorithms that push creators' content in the same fashion. So, we're constantly bombarded, for several hours a day, with content that plucks on our heart strings of desire. We're told how there's a solution for things we never imagined as problems. We're "educated" on why our exercise routines aren't getting us results. We're shown the thousands of customers that are finally happy because they bought some newfangled gadget.

What does this do?

It creates a feeling that we're missing something in our lives. It points to the void within us and says, "If you just have this...that will go away." So, we buy, buy, and buy!!!

We chase instant gratification.

When the deep, meaningful work of traversing challenges in relationships, building a business, training to become a better athlete, or spending hours a day to perfect an art—when the prospect of that arises, we give up too early, we don't fail enough, or we barely get started on what we say we want because it's not as easy as hitting the BUY button.

When it comes to truly overcoming depression by developing healthy habits, challenging our own mindsets, and confronting the past pain, many of us are left ill-equipped for the idea of what any kind of long-term journey looks like. The only way to equip ourselves is having the knowledge that we've been trained for instant gratification and knowing that it's going to take courage, willpower, and tenacity to break through to do the deep work that our life deserves.

Anyway... On that note, this is not about making you not depressed next month or in three months or in six months. This is a long-term game of you building yourself into the person that you want to be, the person that is generally happy, confident, able to communicate easily, can draw boundaries in relationships, and of course, can go after and get anything that they want in their life.

This is about building you into that person.

This depression is just letting you know right now that you're not the person that you want to be. It's letting you know that you've been hurt, and you need to confront that pain. Look, I know it doesn't seem like it but you are in a beautiful place in your life because you have a decision that you can make right here to start playing that long-term game. You actually have to think of it in the long-term because if you think about it in the day-to-day, your depressive mind is going to take over and will to sabotage this whole process. It's going to say, "This is not going to work. You're an idiot. You're stupid. You're not good enough. What's the point? Nothing ever works. This isn't going to help me. Everything goes wrong for me. I've tried things like this before. It's not going to happen."

That's what your depressive mind is going to tell you, and if you view it on a day-to-day basis and get into that short-term goal mindset, the depression will sabotage this. For now, you have to get your mind into a long-term oriented position and understand that you're building structures that are going to draw you into a future that you deserve. It's like putting your healing on autopilot because once you build these structures into your life and develop courage, not only is your courage muscle going to be so strong that you can just overcome anything but you're going to have a slew of healthy habits in your life that keep you emotionally, mentally, and physically regulated and strong.

The habits themselves are going to vary from person to person because some of these habits that I'm going to suggest are ones you may already have built into your life. Therefore, they won't develop your courage muscle because there isn't anything to overcome. Some of these habits may come more naturally and easily to some than others. Some people love exercising, and some people hate it, so the people that hate it are really going to benefit from exercising because it's going to develop that courage muscle. It doesn't mean that if you really hate a specific type of exercise, you should go and do it if it's going to make you more miserable.

If you dislike or feel resistance in going to the gym, but when you come back from the gym, you feel good and you like that feeling, then that's what you want to go after. If you go to the gym but hate going to the gym and you come back and still hate everything about the experience, then maybe going to the gym isn't for you. You have to use your discretion. You have to use your understanding of yourself to choose habits that are going to help you build courage but also not make you miserable.

How Long It Takes to Build a Habit

There is a myth floating around that if you do something every day for 21 days, 3 weeks, then it will automatically become a regular practice in your life. But, there is science that shows that building habits can be different for different people. Not only that but different habits can take a longer or short period to build. The range is between 18 and 254 days, but on average, people solidify practices into habits around the 66-day mark. This is really great science to go off of, and in my experience, this is certainly true.

My background in traditional martial arts often taught me to practice certain forms or exercises in 100-day cycles, which is very traditional. One of the qi gong forms I learned was traditionally practiced over a 100-day cycle—every day for 100 days. If you missed a day, you began again. I did this with multiple forms of this qi gong set, and the transformation was powerful. This kind of depth with one practice created the space for very profound changes to occur. I believe part of the profound impact that this had on my body and mind was due to having to do it every day for a hundred days without stopping. There is some kind of madness that sets in during the final 30 days. Overcoming all of the mind's diversionary tactics and reasons why not to continue takes a lot of willpower. It's a very deep level of courage building.

The length shows you your ability to control your mind and your actions, and that builds a lot of confidence in your ability. I wouldn't recommend putting yourself through this kind of gauntlet from the get-go because it may have the effect of setting you back instead of moving you forward. Doing something every day for 100 days is intense!

To begin layering these habits, I recommend a period between 30 and 90 days to establish a habit before moving on to the next habit. Part of this process is getting to know yourself better. So, feel it out. Different practices may take more or less time to establish. As you add the next habit, take a week to check in with yourself. Is the first habit faltering under the weight of adding another? Do you need more space with the first? Is the first actually still challenging you and developing your courage muscle?

If in the future you want to seriously challenge yourself, then choose a practice and attempt to do a 100-day cycle where you never miss a day. Give it go, but for now, start slow. Remember, this is about building courage, so we have to start with low lifts before we go on to the heavier lifts. At the end of this chapter, there is an assessment you can use to guage whether or not you're ready to move on to the next habit.

Habit #1: Make Your Bed

In our society, when you think about some of the most courageous warriors, your mind will probably go to Navy SEALs. Their training is the most rigorous training that turns human beings into unstoppable warriors by developing their bodies and minds with incredible physical power and mental fortitude.

Where does it all start?

Making their beds.

You've probably heard of the book or a least the concept from Admiral William McRaven, a former Navy SEAL. In his book, *Make Your Bed: Small things that can change your life...and maybe the world*, McRaven shows that starting the day with a small task like making your bed instills discipline, pride, and a sense of accomplishment. It establishes a positive mindset and sets the tone for the day. This simple act is the cornerstone to success.

When I started fighting back against depression, one of the first things that actually made a difference was taking care of my house and personal hygiene and making sure I showered, brushed my teeth, and stuff like that.

It began with making my bed because there's something that happens when you wake up and the first thing that you do is something that you don't want to do, like making your bed. For most, when we wake up, we don't want to start our day with a choice. For starters, maybe you want to get coffee, a cigarette, something sweet, or check social media. Whatever it is, whatever your normal routine is, most people don't want to make their beds.

Remember, taking action "doing something you don't want to do" is going to activate and build your courage muscle. Making your bed is the first habit that I would recommend to start building into your life. It's super simple. It's super easy. It takes you about 37 seconds of your day to make your bed, but it'll change how you think and how you feel.

That little, tiny action will make a big difference.

You're going to do that for 30-90 days until it becomes a habit before moving onto the next thing. Now, I habitually make my bed. I make my bed every morning. Most mornings, I still don't want to do it, but it's hardwired into me and it makes me feel good. So, the feeling of not wanting to make your bed may never go away, but you'll be good to move on to your second habit somewhere in that 30-90 day window. Trust yourself—you'll know.

Habit #2: Keep It Clean

The second practice that I recommend adding is personal and domestic hygiene. This is really an extension of making your bed. People with depression struggle with this because apathy completely takes over. It takes you over, tells you you're worthless, and tells you that nothing matters, so why would you shower? Why would you brush your teeth? Why would you exercise? Why would you eat decent foods? It doesn't matter. It's all pointless. It's all useless, right?

Here's what I mean when I say keep it clean.

Personal Hygiene:

Brush your teeth and floss

Shower regularly

Clip your nails

Get haircuts

Domestic Hygiene:

Do the dishes

Keep up with laundry

Vacuum and mop

Keep your place organized

Clean your bathroom

Declutter

You might be reading this section thinking, "I bought a book about overcoming depression, and now I'm being told to clean my house and take a shower."

When your space is in disarray, you're in disarray. If you are gross and unkept, you're going to feel worse about yourself internally. Your body and living space is a reflection of how you feel about yourself. Sometimes, you have to fake it until you make it. In this case, you need to start showing yourself some love through these two practices. You might not feel much love towards yourself at all right now. It's probably the exact opposite—I know what it feels like to hate yourself. Like I've mentioned before, The Courage Method isn't all about fighting and battling. There's a huge part of this that is going to require you to get in touch with your softer and gentler side. It's one of the reasons you're in this situation. You haven't been allowed to access that side of yourself. Keeping your body and surroundings clean are two practical ways that you can begin to show yourself some love. It's like a chicken-and-the-egg situation. What comes first? Feeling love for yourself then showing it, or showing yourself love then feeling it?

It sounds like a rhetorical question, but it's not.

Here's the answer. Depression doesn't want you to show yourself love. It thrives in the darkness of loneliness, self-hatred, confusion, and doubt. When taken over by that, you'll never magically start feeling love for yourself so that you can finally show yourself some. It's just not going to happen that way. By showing yourself love, you create light, a light where depression cannot survive. The depressive mind can easily turn this into another chore, and when you don't complete it, you'll be punished. This is not a chore but an act of resistance against the depressive mind that searches for way to abuse you. It's a reflection of the pain you endured but did not resolve.

These will be small acts of self-love, a way to build courage, and a way to improve how you feel about yourself and the place you live. Additionally, there's power in the simplicity of momentum. Making your bed and keeping it clean are the smaller wins that will start to create momentum in the process of creating and layering habits. There's power in the simplicity of momentum. They will feed you with the energy you need to create bigger wins, not just in building more healthy habits but also later in the method when you start to gather your party, learn to navigate emotions, surrender your pain, and prioritize your path and purpose.

Habit #3: Freeze Your Dick Off

Cold water calls your name.

My search for a way out of depression brought me to some strange places and practices. Some I won't even mention in this book because they were complete dead ends, but one that was strange and I found deeply beneficial is cold exposure. It's in the ethos now, and it seems like everyone is talking about it. Cold exposure practices have existed for thousands of years across cultures, including the Greeks, indigenous peoples of America and Scandinavia, and countless other cultures.

It was part of my kung fu training, and I rediscovered it later in life through Wim Hof's book *The Way of the Iceman*. In my kung fu training, it had to be one of my least favorite things to do, and it's why I still practice it today.

I remember the first day we had to jump in the snowy creek. We started off with an hour of intense conditioning to warm up our bodies followed by two-person drills conditioning our forearms for striking and then shirtless qi gong in the sun. The last part wasn't bad because we'd already been training, and although cold, it was generally relaxing. I remember thinking "This wasn't half bad. The training was hard, but I feel good, and this is a nice way to end the session."

Wrong.

Then, my sifu said, "Alright, get in the water."

Never having got in water colder than 68 degrees Fahrenheit, I was confused.

It was about 35 degrees out. Wasn't an hour or so in those temperatures without a coat enough to build an "indomitable spirit?"

We waded into the water, and everything in my body said to get out. I kept walking. At about chest height, I started to uncontrollably hyperventilate. At neck height, fear peaked. After totally submerging myself, my body screamed.

I burst through the surface in a panic.

My sifu said, "Breathe deep. Control your body."

I gasped for air, attempting to slow my breathing. My body burned with freezing pain.

I never knew cold water could feel like pain.

Eventually, I gained control of my breath. I sensed the pain around me and focused on letting go and relaxing.

My sifu said, "Now, go to the bottom. Dig your hands into the bottom of the creek and stay as long as you can."

I took a huge breath and submerged myself, swimming to the bottom and sinking my hands into the freezing mud.

A silence and peace came over me like never before.

It was just a sense of nothingness.

I re-emerged from the water, swam to shore, grabbed a towel, and felt the most alive I ever had in my life.

"What the hell did I just do?"

Years later, when I rediscovered this practice in my depressive years, it was a life saver. It helped me remember how strong I was, and as I started to practice it again, it was a key factor in rebuilding my courage and my willpower.

I highly recommend making this part of your life. It's a little more on the intense side of these habits, but for men, that physical intensity is important. You can start by taking short, 30-second cold showers at the end of your shower. Do it every day. Slowly build up to 2-minute periods with your shower at the coldest setting. Studies have shown that only 11 minutes a week of cold water exposure will increase dopamine levels in your body. Dopamine is a neurotransmitter that helps regulate your mood and is capable of enhancing focus, attention, and goal-directed behavior. Having more of that in your life will help you overcome depression by improving your mood and increasing feelings of motivation.

This isn't just about releasing feel-good chemicals. This is a great practice for developing your courage muscle because for most of us—it's not comfortable. You are doing something that is outside of your comfort zone, and it requires you to activate the anterior mid-cingulate cortex, helping you to develop courage. What's more, this is about gaining control over your response to life stressors. Without training, cold water exposure is very stressful on your body. Your body will start to shiver, you'll start to hyperventilate, and at some temperatures, it can feel almost painful. If you can gain control of your breath, keep your mind focused, and relax, you'll build resilience to stress and control over your automatic response.

This gives you the tools to cope with emotional upsets, triggers, and depressive episodes in a whole new way. Instead of being dominated by the response you body has, you'll be able to gain control of your breath, keep your mind focused, and relax. This is just the beginning. In Chapter 7.6, you'll learn the technique for taking this a step further by letting go of the pain that sits suppressed at the bottom of this depression.

Start your day by making your bed, taking care of a few house chores, showering, and finishing with the most uncomfortable, freezing, cold shower. This will start your day with courage-building practices—all showing that you care about yourself.

Habit #4: Move Your Body

Oftentimes, a diet and exercise go hand in hand, and people generally work these habits in tandem. If you've never attempted to alter your diet or do any kind of regular exercise, then I recommend that you choose one to focus on first. Start with whichever one is going to be easier. Remember that our primary goal is building courage. We're working up to higher and higher levels of resistance. Just like at the gym, you would start with a 10-pound weight then move to 15, 25, 35, 40, etc. You want to pick what's going to be the easiest but still offers resistance and then save the other one for later, whether it's a diet or exercise.

Let's talk about my personal favorite first: exercise. Finding the right exercise for you is critical in this process. Not only is regular exercise shown to induce an influx of many good-feeling endorphins but it's an extremely powerful tool in building courage.

The 3 Must-Haves in an Exercise Practice

1. You enjoy doing it.
2. You are always challenged and growing.
3. A guide, a trainer, or a mentor.

These are my 'rules,' so to speak, when it comes to choosing the right type of exercise for you. If you're like me and the thought of going to the gym to run on a treadmill for 45 minutes sounds like Satan's torture device, then don't do that. Find something that you can get excited about that actually brings you some excitement and dare I say... joy. You also want something where you're constantly challenging yourself. That's why I'm a big fan of martial arts because I always feel like whenever I go to train, I'm being challenged. Plus, I'm learning to use my body in new and unique ways and learning to defend myself. I see a lot of guys really benefit from going to the gym to focus on strength training because it offers that level of challenge and growth.

The third part, which we'll talk more in depth about in the coming chapters, is getting support in this area, whether it is a personal trainer, a martial arts teacher, a yoga teacher, a cycling class instructor, or even a rock climbing gym with some people that are more experienced. The key is to find someone to support your growth.

I would have never done all of that crazy training on my own. It took having someone help me train my mind and body. And, here's the thing. Just because you have someone pushing you to your limit doesn't mean you won't develop courage. If you're being challenged by an exercise, you always have the option to stop, walk away, or quit all together.

If you don't have the funds to put into this, then you can certainly find resources online, and I think a decent replacement would be following someone online that has free YouTube videos that you can follow along with and train with. Having that personalized attention and someone standing over you so you can't cheat on yourself is much more beneficial.

Habit #5: Eat Well

I've tried a lot of different diets. At one point, I was mostly fruitarian. I have tried a vegetarian diet. I have attempted a keto diet. I have done fasting, intermittent fasting, and juice cleanses. I've played with a lot of different things, and what I've come up with is that simplicity and consistency is key. There are a lot of diets and fad diets floating around there that take a tremendous amount of willpower and attention, but if you're not in the head space to take that on, then start by switching to a whole food. Ditch all the processed food.

It's the simplest and most powerful diet change you can make.

Is it easy? Definitely not!

But, it lacks the level of daily scrutiny and research that a lot of other diets require, like weighing and measuring every meal, eating the "right" food groups together, eating the right meals at the right time, eating a certain amount of meals per day and abstaining at other times. The list goes on.

Switching to a whole food diet will get you the most results with the least complexity and still require you to activate the anterior midcingulate cortex. All these other diets no doubt have their place. There may be diets out there that are specific to depression, but if you don't have that type of energy right now and apathy controls your life, just work on switching to a whole food diet.

Start by getting rid of any sugary or highly processed foods, like sodas, chips, cookies, crackers, sugary cereals, frozen meals, and candy. Start by cutting that out of your life and replace it with fruit, vegetables, protein, and whole grains. The biggest percent of your diet will be fruits and vegetables, then your proteins, and finally, dairy and grains. It's very simple. In the resource section, you will find a few books that can help you with building this type of eating habit.

If you want to go deeper later on, you can explore more diets that are going to require you to take action or resist on an even deeper level, and you absolutely should. There's a lot of research that shows that gut health is critical in the production of many of our feel good neurotransmitters. Over time, you will hone in on what works for you, your body, and your lifestyle. Not only are bodies unique in their genetic makeup but we all have different lifestyles that require different levels of nutrition. An olympic athlete is going to have very different needs than someone that works in an office. For now, start easy because if you're eating mostly processed foods or fast foods and you switch to a whole food diet, you're going to start feeling the benefits of that pretty immediately in your body and your mindset.

The Pitfalls of Habit Building

Building habits ain't easy, and that's it. It's going to take continued effort over time. There are going to be times where you get into a great rhythm, other times where you'll completely flop, and some times where you might abandon this quest for weeks at a time. That's just the nature of life, being human, and working on yourself. This isn't going to feel like an eye of the tiger, Rocky Balboa montage. It's not going to feel good or feel cool all the time. It's going to be tough, but the outcomes are well worth the struggle and fight. I want you to prepare for all eventualities on this journey.

It's important to stay focused on the 'why' that's driving you to do this, which is twofold:

1. Building your courage muscle to overcome depression.

2. Adding healthy habits to change the trajectory of your life.

You may have other goals that crop up during this process. It could be losing a little extra weight or attaining a certain physique. It could be that you want to be able to be more confident so you can go after a certain job or partner, but I want you to stay focused on the two reasons above. It's very easy for the mind to distract you and derail this whole process. You'll get all of those desires after you overcome depression. Prioritize building the courage muscle and layering habits now—your future self will thank you.

Habit Layering Assessment:

You can use this assessment when you are unsure of whether or not you are ready to start layering on another habit. This will help you know if a certain practice has turned into a habit. Ask yourself the questions below as prompts to inquire within yourself as to whether you've turned a specific practice into a habit.

1. Have you consistently performed this action for the past 30 days or more?

2. Do you find yourself doing this action without consciously thinking about it?

3. When faced with disruptions or challenges, how likely are you to stick to this behavior?

4. Do you associate positive feelings or a sense of accomplishment with completing this action?

5. Is this behavior seamlessly integrated into a specific time or event in your daily schedule?

6. Can you envision yourself continuing this behavior in the long term?

7. Do you feel prepared to start adding another practice to your routine?

If you answered 'Yes' to five or more of these questions, that's a pretty good signal that you're ready to move on to the next habit. If you answered 'Yes' to four or less of these questions, then give yourself another week or two of practice before revisiting the assessment. In time, you'll develop a more acute internal sense of when you're ready to add another.

The Art of Alchemy

"The self is not something ready-made but something in continuous formation through choice of action."
— John Dewey

CHAPTER 7.6:

Healing Your Pain

You've learned how the depression trap works and what you need to do to build courage to fight apathy. The only thing that is missing is a little magic. The Art of Alchemy is the internal magic you need to disarm your triggers, turn off your automatic emotion suppression system, and heal your trauma.

The Art of Alchemy is the internal process of transforming pain and trauma into understanding, peace, and joy. To make this transformation, the first step is to become emotionally intelligent. Emotional intelligence is the ability to feel, name, and regulate your emotions. This will help you to disarm your automatic emotion suppression system and regulate yourself during and after triggers. The second step is learning how to surrender to heal the pain that you've been suppressing. This will have a powerful healing effect, thus dismantling the whole depression trap, leaving you to live a full life.

This is how the chapter will go:

1. Identify Emotions: Learn how to pause, feel, and reclaim your emotional vocabulary.

2. Emotional Regulation: Learn how to regulate emotions and triggers with breathing and self-care.

3. Deep Surrender: Learn how to use letting go to heal emotional pain and mental anguish.

Identifying Emotions

It's hard enough being a man and being able to identify emotions but to endure chronic depression makes it even more difficult. We aren't allowed, as men, to be able to identify and express the ways we are feeling. If we're too soft, we're told to toughen up, but then when we don't express our feelings, we're told that we need to express ourselves more. It's a catch-22. To add fuel to this fire, the depressive mind makes it even harder to identify emotions. When you've been so sad, apathetic, and numb for so long, your emotional experience of life becomes grayscale. We've been put in a precarious position, and the only way out is by starting to identify the various emotions we feel throughout the day and obtaining some emotional vocabulary.

Black-and-White Thinking

The depressive mind combined with the limited capability we've been given as men to identify emotions leads to black-and-white thinking. We think of our lives or a single day in terms of good or bad. With depression, this mostly turns out to be a bad day regardless of what happened during that day. Here's an example. You have your first cup of coffee for the day and get a quick shot of joy. Later, you see a friend for lunch and you actually have a pretty decent time. You joke and laugh and it feels nice to see someone. After the meet up, you go back to feeling depressed. Small occasions like this happen throughout the day where you feel a variety of emotions. The strange thing is that at the end of the day or at the end of the week, you look back and say that was a bad day. Your depressive mind and lack of ability to identify emotions leaves you with the impression that everything was bad. For me, I would always chalk up those experiences to "faking it."

I'm not saying this to minimize depression but to give you access to another way out. When you're depressed, apathy is not the only emotion that you experience. It's definitely the dominant emotion, but there are other times when you feel a variety of emotions. Your depressive mind just makes it seem worse than it already is.

"How do I get out of black-and-white thinking?"

It starts with pausing. Throughout your day, pause for the variety of feelings that you experience whether they're negative or positive feelings. Just pause and sense that you feel a little different. Especially with negative emotions, it's going to be challenging at first. Your automatic emotion suppression system is going to want to swoop in and push them down, but it just takes a little pause for you to catch them. Once you've caught a feeling, you can swish it around in your heart a little, feeling the sensations and watching your thoughts. Next, try to identify the feeling with a word or two. You can use an emotion wheel like the one below.

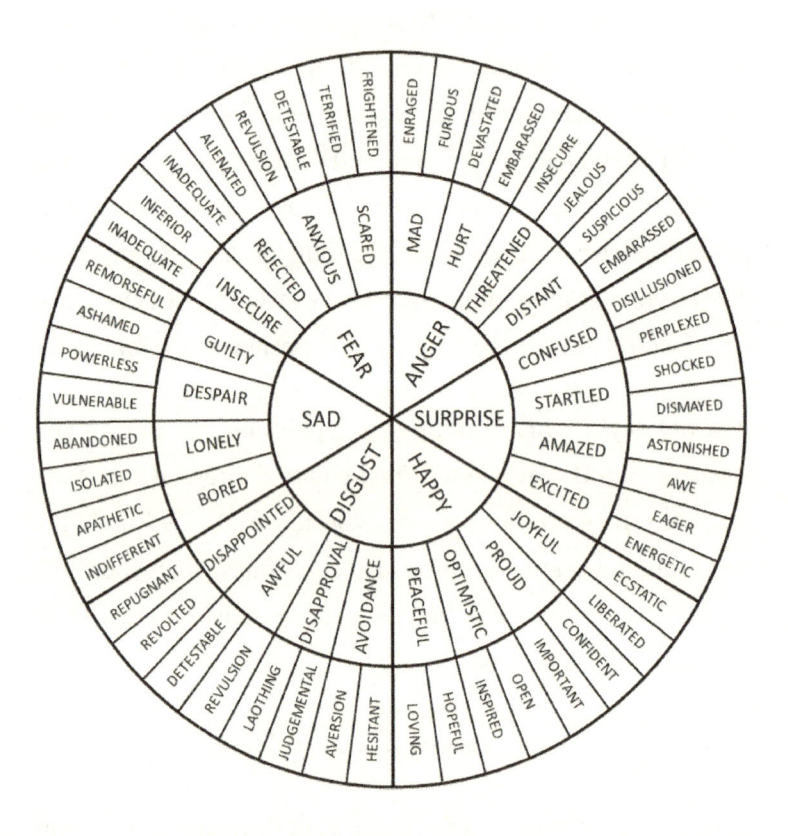

There are dozens of words to describe emotions, and you just lack the words for the complex human emotional experiences you have. The next thing that you'll want to do is keep a record of how you've felt throughout the day. I've recommended a few apps in the resource section for you to check out, but if you want to print out a wheel of emotions and carry around a notebook, have at it. By starting to identify different feelings throughout the day with this new vocabulary and timestamping those moments, you'll start to combat black-and-white thinking. At the end of the day, you'll start to see that you had 7, 8, 9, 10 or up to dozens of different feelings throughout the day. No matter how apathetic you feel, there's no way you can deny the variety of emotions you had. It wasn't a good day or a bad day, but it was a day when you had good times and bad times. When you start to see this, it becomes harder and harder for your depressive mind to dominate your experience.

Emotional Regulation

As you start to identify emotional experiences more and more and build your vocabulary, it makes navigating and regulating your internal world a lot easier. When you feel an emotion arise, you'll have words to identify it. It becomes even harder for that automatic emotions suppression system to push it down.

Why?

When you have vocabulary to identify your emotions, you also have something to do with it. If you feel sad, you can express it by crying. If you feel lonely, you can reach out to a friend. If you feel happy, you can go do something you love or just enjoy it. The struggle of emotions is that they are unknown and come from what feels like the dark depths of our being. It's like a shadow slinking out of a dark cave. No one wants anything to do with that, so just push it back in, right? Right. But, once you have the proper vocabulary, then you'll say, "Oh, that's forlorn. I know exactly what to do with him," or, "Here comes my old pal, contentment. This will be a good time."

This all might sound a bit childish to you, but it's just where we've been left in our emotional development. The more you do this work, the better time you're going to have experiencing and processing the different emotions that come and go in and out of your day.

Navigating Triggers

All of this work isn't just powerful for shutting down your automatic emotion suppression system, dispelling black-and-white thinking, and regulating everyday emotions. It's very powerful for navigating triggers.

We've discussed triggers in depth, and you now know that triggers can bring you back to some of the worst times in your life. It brings up all of the pain and confusion while simultaneously activating your stress response, putting you in a fight-or-flight state. You go from feeling fine to feeling scared, stressed, angry, aggressive, hypervigilant, or sad. The possibilities are endless here.

You've survived those moments, but being able to identify emotions and self-regulate is a complete game changer. Triggered moments start out as complete chaos and then, eventually, they turn into the milieu of emotional experience I just mentioned. Once you're able to identify those emotions, you'll get a better idea of what to do with each one. The stress of those triggers can lessen because you're clear about what's happening and what you're feeling.

The most important thing you can do in these moments as soon as you feel that trigger being pulled is to take space for yourself and start to breathe. Nothing fancy. Just inhale through the nose and exhale out of the mouth. Part of the stress response is an increase in breathing rate and shallow breathing, which further exacerbates feelings of stress and anxiety. This can lead to less oxygen getting to the brain. Since oxygen is crucial for the brain to function optimally, these lowered levels can impair the brain's ability to process emotions and regulate mood. This only adds more fuel to the fire... so we breathe.

Deep breathing gets more oxygen to the brain and also activates the body's rest-and-digest functions. This promotes relaxation and can counteract the stress response. By taking slow, deep breaths, you can signal your body that it's safe to relax.

Start with 10 deep breaths in through your nose and out through your mouth. Then, when you have completed 10 deep breaths, do 10 more, and then another 10, and just keep breathing. The reason I suggest to do them in sets of 10 is so that your mind has something to focus on. Without setting a goal to get to 10, you might only do three or four and get consumed by all the emotions and the physiological symptoms of stress. Counting keeps you focused on breathing which helps your brain and body manage the trigger.

Turning Self-Punishment to Self-Love

We talked about self-punishing thoughts in an earlier chapter as a result of pain being suppressed. These self-punishing thoughts are related to how we have been taught that our emotions are unimportant. We've been told over and over to "man up, shut up, and move on." It's a verbally violent training we've endured and adopted as our own internal voice.

Part of emotional regulation is retraining that voice from being abusive to being loving. You know this self-punishing voice all too well, and it shows up on regular depressive days and intensifies after triggers. It sounds like, "I don't want to be here. I wish I wasn't alive. What's wrong with you? You are worthless. You're such a horrible person. I hate myself. I want to die."

These thoughts are not just painful but completely counter to healing your trauma. They actually wound you further and deepen the pain you already experience. Where do you turn when your mind isn't even on your side?

You turn inward.

Transforming this self-punishing voice is no easy feat; it is deeply ingrained in us. The more we think of it, the easier it is to be thought of again. As you dismantle the depression trap and heal your pain, these voices will in turn get softer and eventually disappear. What will help that process is to start to change your reaction to your own pain and your triggers.

Why kick yourself when you're down?

Why hate yourself when you're having a very human experience and a poor reaction to horrible trauma?

You're not bad. You're not broken. You're not worthless. Getting rid of these self-punishing and self-hating voices starts with just doing the opposite. It starts with recognizing that all of the skills you need to navigate emotions and overcome trauma have never been given to you. Whatever trauma you experienced is not your fault. Your reaction to what happened to you is valid, there's no reason to minimize it. When you start to realize that full story of what you've been put through and realize that it's not your fault, the only logical option is to start giving yourself the love you deserve. You're not the enemy. You're not the problem. You're not bad, or weak, or broken.

Look man, you've got to give yourself a break, and it starts now, not in some distant future when you're healed and happy. When you're depressed, and triggered, and a complete wreck, put your hands on your heart and tell yourself, "I'm sorry. I forgive you. I love you. Thank you."

Say it a hundred times over, and I bet within the first few times, you'll start to cry. When was the last time you gave yourself love? When was the last time you gave yourself the space to be a human? When was the last time you didn't treat yourself like you have to be this perfectly carved, impenetrable statue?

You're human. You have emotions. You have pain. It's all going to be okay.

It starts with putting that self-hating and self-punishing voice that has been trained in you by society to rest and replacing it with a voice that loves you, cares about your well-being, and has your back. Put down the book and say it with me.

"I'm sorry. I forgive you. I love you. Thank you."

Letting Go

You've learned how important it is to feel and identify emotions to dismantle your automatic emotion suppression system. You've also learned how to start working with your triggers in a whole new way to create peace through breathing and healing through self-care. But, what do you do with all the unprocessed emotions? What do you do with the pain from trauma? How do you heal and move on with your life?

When I was doing all of that intense martial arts training, an important component was letting go. That training was more than just about building an indomitable spirit. It was about healing. When I was training, the essence of what my sifu instructed me to do during the intensity was, "Stay present. Relax. Let go." Allow everything that arose to exist without resistance. It was the practice of not suppressing emotions and was a way to dismantle the automatic emotion suppression system.

Think of a jar filled with water and a layer of dirt at the bottom. The dirt is all of the unresolved emotions and pain. The intensity of the training shook up the jar and clouded the water. Now, all of the emotions and pain that were settled at the bottom of the jar were activated and alive in my direct experience. The frustration. The anger. The sadness. All of it. There was only one thing to do—surrender. It was a very purposeful practice of bringing the pain to the surface so there was the opportunity to transform it. Emotions need to be experienced fully, and once you give them the space to do that, they move through you. It's not going to change what happened that caused the trauma but it's going to heal the pain that cries out to be heard.

I'm not saying that you need to go do intense kung fu training to process the pain from your trauma, but there is something that already stirs up that pain. You know what it is—it's the trigger. Everytime you're triggered, you shake up the jar, and everytime that it happens, it is an opportunity to let go of those painful emotions and experiences.

How do you let go?

The term 'letting go' is a little misleading. Many think of it as letting go of pain or negative emotion. The attempt to let go of an experience in this way is actually a rejection of it, and the attempt turns into suppression. You're saying, "I have to let go of this and get it out of my life." None of us want to experience pain, deep sadness, loneliness, or any other negative emotions. We want to feel good—especially when we're suffering from depression, but this way of letting go is not actually letting go.

Letting go is an absolute acceptance of what you're experiencing in the moment. If you're feeling pain, then it is accepting that you're feeling pain. There is no resistance, there is nothing being done, and there is no action. You don't have to do some kind of mantra to dispel the pain. Just be with it and allow it. It's very simple. What complicates the process is the automatic emotion suppression system, the lack of ability to feel and identify feelings, and the fast-paced, goal-driven culture we live in. Our negative emotions and our pain are the enemy of productivity. They're useless for meeting quotas and progressing. They're meaningless when it comes to trying to survive. Even the act of letting go becomes another form of productivity. How much pain did you let go of in the last 30 minutes? Did you meet your 'letting go' goals for the month? Did you use your weekend wisely to let go of enough painful emotions so that you can work better this week and the next?

Do you hear how insane that sounds?

This is the culture we are steeped in. Over and over, in a million different ways, we're told, "Your worth is how much you can produce." I won't go too far down that rabbit hole, but it's a major pitfall when it comes to letting go. It's also part of the reason that you've arrived here in the first place. All of the standards for being a man are about our ability to produce and how much we can cut out for ourselves and our family. Identifying emotions, processing trauma, and letting go of pain are not taught as part of that standard.

Let's return to the question "What is letting go?"

It's a silent curiosity exploring the experience of pain and allowing whatever needs to come forth, to come forth. It may be letting that pain well up in your chest and burst out as the worst and best ugly face cry. It could be anger at the perpetrator that wants to come out as yelling. It might be a deep sense of sadness that collapses your entire body. It's acknowledgement of all the loss you've experienced. In the process of letting go, there is no rejection, judgment, or suppression—for once, just allowing things to be as they are.

Let's be clear. Letting go is not just a spiritual mantra repeated in yoga and meditation classes. It's a deeply profound healing mechanism, so much so that there are entire therapeutic modalities structured around it. Case in point—acceptance and commitment therapy, or ACT. ACT encourages you to accept your thoughts and feelings rather than fight or feel guilty about them. The core idea is that by allowing these emotions to exist without trying to suppress them, you can reduce their emotional impact. It's been proven that ACT can be very effective in reducing symptoms of anxiety, depression, and stress.

Crying

If you can't remember the last time that you cried, then you need to start doing it. Crying helps you release painful emotions and stress. Just like laughter, shouting, and whining, crying is a normal human function for expressing emotion. Obviously, for us guys, crying is not something that is allowed because it is viewed as a form of weakness. But in fact, being able to cry just shows that you're courageous with your emotions, that you're compassionate, and that will make you more happy and relaxed. There's not much more to say about it, but just start doing it. Since it may be a while since you cried, it's going to take some practice to start crying. Music always does it for me. Start crying and let me know how that works out for you.

The Letting Go Technique

Throughout this chapter, we've explored a series of practical techniques that men need to navigate emotions and triggers and to heal from the pain of trauma. This technique brings everything together that you've learned into a simple 4-step process that you can use in multiple ways. You can use it when you're feeling a difficult emotion, when you're triggered, when you're feeling depressed, or after an argument. The list goes on. This is going to be your go-to technique for everything emotional on your journey in overcoming depression.

Step 1: Pause

Take a moment to acknowledge and name what you're feeling. Use the wheel of emotions or your app to identify the feeling if you're confused.

Step 2: Breathe

Whether you're triggered, feeling depressed, or feeling a difficult emotion, start breathing. Take medium to slow breaths in through the nose and out through the mouth. Start with ten, then do another ten. Keep going until you feel yourself start to relax.

Step 3: Let Go

Let go of all resistance to the experience and be present with it. Surrender and let your heart and body do what they need to do. Especially with these painful experiences. Don't resist, just let it exist within you.

Step 4: Take Care

The feeling may not fade instantly, so just stick with it and take care of yourself. Don't be harsh. Don't self-punish. Don't judge. Give yourself the self-love you need. "I'm sorry. I forgive you. I love you. Thank you." If you feel like you need to take action, then go for walk, listen to music, stretch, take a bath, write, or call a friend.

This simple process will not only give you enhanced emotional intelligence and the ability to identify and regulate your emotional states but it will help you move through the pain caused by your trauma. It takes tremendous courage to lean into your emotional experiences instead of suppressing them. Once you do, you'll discover that they are not even as half as scary or confusing as you may have made them out to be. You'll move through negative states quicker. As the process of letting go dissolves your pent up emotions and pain, you will start to transform into a lighter, more relaxed, and authentically happy person.

The Art of Help

"You are the average of the five people you spend the most time with."
— Jim Rohn

CHAPTER 7.7:

Gathering Your Party

I want to kick off this chapter by saying good job. Those last few chapters were a long haul. I'm sure that there were many moments of reflection that may not have brought up the best feelings. The whole journey of internal work and self-discovery is filled with moments of discomfort, whether it's looking at the past or experiencing pain in the present. You'll experience times of doubt and confusion, and you'll wonder, "Is it all worth it? Will this ever be complete?" The answer is yes. It is worth it. Over time, things will even out, the lows will be softer and become more manageable, and the good times will be more prevalent. It takes consistent effort over time.

This leads us perfectly to the *Art of Help*, learning who to surround yourself with and how to do it. This journey is perilous, and like every hero on a journey to do battle, he must gather his ragtag but loyal party. You will learn about the 4 party members that are required for your journey.

See, the journey out of depression is not one to go alone. You're well aware of the internal mechanism of your enemy by now. You're developing some fighting capability and techniques for transforming pain, but there are times where you'll feel overtaken, tired, weakened, confused, and apathetic. This is why it's so important to have people around you that are going to support you through those times without judgment. In studies on adversity, there has been one resounding element that has been an indicator of resilience. It wasn't just individual willpower but was support. Those who had the proper support systems were better equipped and more likely to overcome adversity, whether it was external or internal.

In this chapter you're going to learn about:

- The 4 party members you'll need to develop courage, heal trauma, and become a stronger version of yourself.

- Why you absolutely need support in multiple forms to get through this depression.

- The #1 most important party member that you cannot do without.

- How to develop deeper relationships with the people in your life.

The Four Party Members

As we go through the list of people that you need to help you through this depression, I want you to take mental notes. Ask yourself if you have this person in your life already, or if not, start to explore who could be this person for you. There's a pretty good chance that you already have some of these characters lying in wait in your life. You just need to call on them for support.

The one rule I want you to follow as you gather your party is to choose people that are going where you want to go or are already where you want to be. You want to surround yourself with people that are going to help you build a new future. It doesn't mean they have to be perfect, but you want people that are going to reinforce the new version of yourself that you're building. It's very easy to get stuck in depression when you're surrounded by people whose own negativity keeps you down.

1. Trusted Advisor

This is your right hand man, your best friend, and someone that you can talk through anything with, express yourself openly, not be judged, and get feedback when necessary. After getting out of high school or college, and settling down, finding and developing male friendships like this can be challenging, which goes back to the social standards that have been imposed on us guys.

We're taught that we shouldn't need close relationships like this and that we should be able to handle life ourselves and be this impenetrable statue, someone that is a rock for everyone else in our life but who cannot afford to be soft, vulnerable, and essentially human.

This alone makes it near impossible for men to connect with other men. If we all interact through this guise of not needing or wanting support, it leaves us all isolated to deal with the challenges of life alone. This social conditioning is so deep that you may be reading this thinking, "Maybe other guys need that, but that's not me. I'm good."

I suggest you peer a little deeper underneath that layer.

You'll probably find that you're actually not okay with the loneliness and the isolation, even though that's what you've been told being a "strong man" is. To me, being a strong man is being vulnerable and real about your very human feelings. Stuffing them down and ignoring what you need is weakness. It's bowing down to the fear of confronting uncertainty, pain, and your own need for deep and fulfilling relationships—specifically with other men.

That fear has been installed in our hearts by society. It has told us that if we go there, we'll be perceived as weak, as too feminine, or as inadequate.

It's all fear.

This is the block that you're going to have to overcome to either find or further develop this relationship with someone you already know. Again, this is why we train the courage muscle. In endeavoring to build this relationship, there are going to be moments of resistance. The more the courage muscle is developed, the easier it will be to take action.

As you read, you've fallen into one of two camps. You already have a best friend, or you don't have someone you would consider your best friend.

If you have a best friend, the relationship has depth, and you're able to be vulnerable and get the support you need—excellent. But, in my experience, I've had a lot of what I would consider close friends or even best friends, but they still had this superficial quality. This is a by-product of our social conditioning. For us, being close to another guy is being 10 feet away. One way you can develop this friendship is by starting to be open about what you're going through, challenges in your relationship, or whatever you're getting after in your life. Start to name what you're feeling—sadness about your relationship, fear about finances, or worry about your future. Start opening the door of emotionality because the truth is... your buddy actually needs the same thing.

Sometimes, it might even require a more straightforward approach. If you're like me, it would come out as, "Hey man, I need to talk about the shit that's been going on in my life, and it's going to be a little emotional. Can I talk to you about that stuff?"

If you get shut down, then look elsewhere. Don't be open with people that aren't going to be receptive. You have to be a little selfish right now. If your buddy isn't on that level, that's okay, but you need to find this type of relationship for you right now.

This brings us to the second camp of people: you don't have someone you would consider your best friend, or you just found out the person you thought was your best friend isn't.

Go get 'em, champ. Get yourself out there, just be yourself, and never be afraid to be the initiator. It doesn't have to be this awkward conversation like you're hitting on them, and you probably never even have to say, "Want to be my friend?" You just need to start spending time with like-minded guys and let things develop. Let me reiterate at this point that a deep male bond is an absolute requirement for men, not just to overcome depression but to get through life and to be heard and understood as a man—it's very healing and empowering. It's also going to make you feel a lot less isolated and alone.

Start getting out as much as possible and doing things that you like to do. Take a moment to think about the things that you like to do or would like to start doing, or if you're looking to start building the exercise habit, this is a great time to start exploring different avenues. I've found a tremendous amount of connectedness and camaraderie through the outlets that I'm most passionate and excited about: martial arts and writing. I've made life-long friends, and it's those people who have helped me become who I am today. I've heard it said that we are a combination of our five closest friends. Surround yourself with people that you want to be more like. Surround yourself with people who are also pulling themselves together, who want to be better and grow on a personal level.

You typically can find those people in exercise programs, whether it's the gym, martial arts classes, yoga, mountain biking, hiking, rock climbing, or sports clubs. The list goes on. There might be other passions that interest you that you may already be involved in or want to start to explore. It could be woodworking, tabletop games, writing, music, crafting, camping, or maybe it's civil war reenactments. Whatever it is for you, follow it for two reasons. One, to find your trusted advisor and two, because you're interested in doing it and it's going to bring you joy and more reasons to fight like hell to get out of this depression.

2. The Backups

In addition, to your trusted advisor, you'll need a few other people that you can go to for support. This is your second string. Your trusted advisor is going to be someone you feel really comfortable sharing the deep stuff with and is hopefully someone that feels comfortable sharing with you as well. But, you don't want to over rely on that person for everything. You want to have a few people that you can ping-pong between in times of need. It's very easy for the depressive mind to guide you towards isolation. Having several backups can help prevent your depressive mind from tricking you into believing that you are a burden to the people in your life. If you only reach out for help to each person a few times a month, are you really a burden?

I want you to also start identifying people in your life that you would consider your backups. This is an array of people that could be family members, partners, friends, or people from the community or your religious affiliations if any. I'm sure that you will start to see that you have some people in your life that are around to support you. If not, I would suggest taking a deeper look. You may not consider any people in your life backups for a number of reasons. I would investigate those reasons and see if they are valid. Maybe they are, and maybe they're not. If you're still left with a list you're unsatisfied with, then refer back to my suggestion for finding a trusted advisor.

There's a good chance that the people on your list of backups might not know what's going on with you. There's a good chance that they probably do want to know and want to be able to be there for you. That's your next move, letting them know you're going through a hard time and that you're not okay.

Fear of vulnerability and the requirement to be a strong man is the reason that you haven't filled them in yet. It's going to take that courage muscle to break through fear and start talking unabashedly. I know that you can pick up the phone and share with a few of the people in your life that you're struggling. It isn't easy at first, but eventually, you will not care. With practice, you'll care less about what people think or about the perception of your masculinity. Remember, it's actually the most masculine thing you can do to be vulnerable and real with the people in your life. You'll get to the other side of this, and it's the little actions and consistent effort over time that will get you there.

3. Trainer

In conjunction with the exercise habit, I highly recommend that you find someone we'll call your trainer. Just like my martial arts training and just like those montages in kung fu films, you need a sifu, a teacher, or someone to guide you in your chosen exercise practice. A lot of my courage was built through my martial arts training and only intensified by going through the gauntlet of depression. Just like finding the right exercise practice for you, you'll also need to shop around for the right trainer.

I'm always going to recommend martial arts for guys who want to develop courage. Whether it's kung fu, jiu jitsu, MMA, or otherwise, martial arts always pushes you out of your comfort zone and shows you your true potential. There is something visceral and empowering about martial arts. Specifically for depression, to see yourself be able to physically fight only emboldens you to master the garbage in your mind. Martial arts also covers a lot of the recommendations from this methodology. You can find your trainer, your backups, and an exercise practice that encourages you to improve your diet and teaches you to be a fighter.

Here's the one myth I want to break about martial arts studios. Don't be intimidated. I've spent a lot of time in and out of many different types of martial arts studios. For a beginner, it might seem intimidating because everyone knows so much more than you, everyone seems so tough, and there's the looming awkwardness of having to get physical with another guy. But, it's all in your head. Everyone that was in there at one point was a beginner, and I've found that martial arts practitioners are the most generous and down-to-earth people. If you've ever had that desire to try it, then smash through the hesitation, activate your anterior midcingulate cortex, and go after it.

Enough with my martial arts plug. You may be wondering, "Do I absolutely need a trainer?"

The answer is yes, and here's why...

A trainer is going to push you right to your limit and then a little bit beyond that. This is going to consistently activate that anterior midcingulate cortex to help build your courage muscle. Do you think if I didn't have my sifu standing over me saying, "keep going," that I would have done all of that crazy training that was *way* out of my comfort zone? Certainly not, and I wouldn't have reaped the benefits of it. With all of that courage built, I am very easily able to make myself do things that I don't want to do. A trainer is going to keep the bar just above your head so that you keep developing. Chances are they aren't going to be thinking about developing your courage muscle. They're going to be focused on making you better at martial arts, rock climbing, weight lifting, running, or whatever you choose. In the process of your physical development, courage development occurs. Seeing yourself grow in that way is also going to give you a lot more confidence.

Having a trainer doesn't always mean finding a one-on-one trainer. I understand that it can get pretty pricey. If you don't have the funds to do it now, then don't stretch yourself thin. You've got a lot going on, and there's no need to add additional stress. Most martial arts studios are set up as group training, which helps lower the cost. It's not going to be as cheap as a gym membership, but it's definitely going to be better than one-on-one training. A lot of training gyms also offer group sessions or semi-privates. When I was in a tough spot financially, I just went on YouTube and found someone that I liked learning from, which is how I got into strength training with dumbbells. It's not as ideal as having someone there to push you on a session-to-session basis, but work with what you've got—even if it's working out in your living room with YouTube. In that case, always make sure that you push yourself. Without the accountability of someone there watching you, it might be easy to dip out when the going gets tough. Remember what you're doing this for. It's not the 6-pack abs. It's to build courage, and that takes crossing that line from the comfortable to the uncomfortable over and over again.

4. Therapist

You need a therapist. You absolutely need a therapist if you're going to overcome this depression. There are a lot of reasons that guys don't go to therapy. Three of the most common ones are the social stigma surrounding therapy, people thinking they don't need a therapist, and the cost. We'll cover the first two now. In Chapter 11, I'll give you a step-by-step plan for paying and finding a therapist. If you don't think you need a therapist, I hope I can change your mind or, at the very least, I hope we've built enough trust that you'll give it a shot.

The Social Stigma of Therapy

The crazy thing is that a social stigma around therapy still exists. Half of the global population will struggle with mental health at some point in their lives. It's really no different than the physical ailments we develop, and it should be approached as such. Of course, as men, we have an additional level of stigma and resistance we have to overcome in starting therapy. At this point, you're probably starting to see the trend here. Again and again, we're thwarted by our social conditioning of what it means to be a man. That conditioning directly impacts our mental and emotional health and our ability to navigate adversity and heal from trauma. It's no different here. Since getting a therapist is so critical to your healing, you need a mental defense against this social stigma.

I want you to approach the idea of going to therapy as if you've broken a bone. The truth is that there is no difference. There was a traumatic incident that caused pain and changed something structurally in your body. In one case, it's a bone and in the other, it's your brain. As we've learned, the brain is something you can heal just like a broken bone. With a broken bone, you wouldn't leave it be and hope it works itself out. You wouldn't walk it off. You wouldn't man up and deal with the pain. No. You'd get over to the hospital or urgent care and get it fixed. Think of healing from trauma and overcoming depression in the same way! Don't stuff down the pain, ignore the damage, and expect to live life like normal.

Go get help.

If anyone in your life makes an unhelpful comment about you going to therapy, then you can explain this to them. You really shouldn't have to defend yourself or feel bad or uncomfortable about going to therapy, but it's where we're at right now. I've used this line of thinking to defend my actions and have often convinced others that they, too, need to go to therapy!

It's perceived that going to a therapist is a sign of weakness. In fact, it's a tremendous sign of strength to be able to acknowledge that you need help and are going to get it.

Why You Need a Therapist

We've explored all the types of support that you need to overcome depression in this chapter. Support from a therapist is very different. You need someone that is an outsider to your life that is dedicated to just helping you process trauma and your feelings. It's going to take some time to develop trust with this person, but once you do, they become an amazing asset in your life. There are things that I've said to therapists that I have never said to anybody in my life. Once I said them, they were out of my head and stopped causing me fear, anxiety, and suffering. There are different types of therapists who use different approaches and modalities. In the resources section, I provide a list of the different modalities. You can explore them more deeply for yourself. What's even more important than the specific modality is that you have a therapist and that you feel good sharing with them.

When working with a therapist, you'll typically start with more superficial feelings and getting-to-know you type stuff. As the relationship and trust deepens, so will the content.

You'll be able to share more fully and talk about the trauma that you've experienced. In all of this sharing, some really powerful transformations can happen. Just speaking your feelings and thoughts to someone who is truly listening can transform your internal environment. It's like taking off all the heavy weight you've been carrying around, all of the pain, the confusion, and the sadness. As you begin to unload the emotions and tell your stories, you'll start to get a new view of your life narrative. You'll start to see the ways in which the depressive mind may be manipulating your experiences. You'll start to unravel connections you've never noticed before, identify triggers that are causing deeper depressive episodes, and process the intense pain that lives within you.

This is not a linear process. It's circular. It spirals. It's messy and confusing, and you can't do it alone. Each time you go and do this work with your therapist, you'll be lightening the load and untangling the web of trauma, pain, and emotion. Like with many things found in my methodology, you have to think of the long-term implications of doing therapy. It took years and years, maybe decades, to get you to where you are today. It's going to take time to unravel, but with consistency, it will happen. Talking about trauma and revealing your inner world to someone isn't fun. It can be hard to confront. Sometimes, there will be weeks where you can't wait to go to therapy and other days you'll show up with no desire to be there—both are okay. It requires courage to keep going back, to keep going deeper, and to keep doing this work.

Navigating the Therapeutic Relationship

1. Be in communication

Communicate with your therapist about what you need and what you're looking for. Some people need therapists to just listen, and others need more nudging and support navigating the inner webs of the mind. You might want exercises and worksheets to bring home to practice during the week, or you may hate the idea of that. Be clear about what you want, but also put some trust in your therapist's ability to see what you need. Always be upfront about how you're feeling. If you're going too deep too fast, then ask to slow the roll. If there are certain topics your therapist nudges at but you're not ready to talk about, then tell them. Digging into the depths of your heart, mind, and soul can be complicated and confusing, so just be in communication throughout.

2. Move on when ready

I've had multiple therapists throughout my life. Some were excellent, and others were not what I needed. Each of those therapists served a certain purpose in my growth and healing. One of my therapists was on the more existential side of things and allowed me to talk almost the whole time. He just listened. Here and there, he would give me little nudges and ideas. This allowed me to really follow all the strings of the webs of my mind from past to present and back again. This helped me rewrite the narrative of my life from the strict binary of good and bad to something more complex and down-to-earth. Then, there was another therapist who brought out worksheets, spoke about therapeutic concepts, and gave me homework. This was more structured but allowed me to understand the inner workings of my mind and start to rewire ways of thinking. I stayed with both for over a year, and I was able to heal a lot of emotional pain, which is required to dismantle the depression trap. There were other therapists that only lasted a few months or even weeks. I knew the relationship wasn't right, and I didn't feel like I'd get what I needed, so I moved on. That's the lesson here. Stay for however long you need, and move on when you feel it's the right time.

3. They're not all good

Just like there are bad cops, bad teachers, and bad janitors, there are bad therapists. I don't want that to deter you from getting a therapist because you absolutely need a therapist. There was one therapist who, within two weeks, diagnosed me with major depressive disorder, general anxiety disorder, and post traumatic stress disorder and sent me to a psychiatrist who said I had attention deficit disorder. I had this feeling that there was so much wrong with me, and it was discouraging to say the least. Then, for our next session, they didn't show up. This was during the midst of COVID, so we were only doing remote sessions via telehealth. I sat there staring at an empty screen for 15 minutes, prepared to spill my guts, severely depressed, and suicidal. I prepared all week for everything that I wanted to talk about. I felt abandoned and hurt. It was through a larger practice, and when I called the office, they said the therapist had quit a week earlier. They gave me no notice of this and didn't set me up with an alternative. I didn't give them a chance to remedy the situation because I had lost trust with them. It's an important lesson that I hope you can learn from me. Be selfish. This is about you and your healing. Know that not every therapist or organization is going to be able to help you, but don't let it be an excuse not to get help. Fight for what you deserve, and don't stay in therapeutic relationships that do not help you or potentially hurt you.

Hopefully at this point, you're convinced that getting a therapist is a crucial part of your healing process. Smashing through the social stigma and figuring out how you're going to find and pay for a therapist can feel like a lot of work. If you're worried about what people will think, just remember that this is your journey and this is for you. Oftentimes, when I began new things or changed life directions, there were certain people in my life that only questioned and doubted what I was doing. They were the same people that, once I was successful in that change, became my biggest cheerleaders. It's obvious now that those people were just projecting their own fears onto me. Do not allow the people in your life or society to project any of their fears or doubts on you. Be strong and committed to yourself. Remember, you're doing this for yourself. As for finding and paying for a therapist, in Chapter 11, I provide a quick, step-by-step guide that will help you do it in 30 days or less.

CHAPTER 7.8:

Audentis Fortuna Iuvat

You've just learned the entirety of The Courage Method. It has everything that you need to overcome depression once and for good. I've said over and over again that it's going to take consistent effort over time. You're not just overcoming depression and healing from trauma. The Courage Method is the process of undoing decades of social conditioning, unwinding trauma, and rebuilding yourself into the man you want to be. The third and final part of this book is all about helping you get started on your first few steps. I want to help you start to build some momentum and understand that you're completely capable of going on this journey.

All you need to do is take action over and over again.

One of my biggest frustrations during my depression was the saying, "It's going to get better," because that was bull. I don't blame them, but the truth is they didn't know what to say and just wanted me to feel better. They wanted the old, optimistic Dylan to come back. They didn't want to hear the ways in which I hated myself or how I wanted to die.

I would always ask, "How?"

I never got a comprehensive answer because we're just not equipped as a society to deal with pain or trauma. We're stripped of our processes and rituals for grieving, feeling, and transforming. So look, I wish I could tell you that everything is going to be okay and that this is all going to get better in time.

But, the truth is... it's not going to get better.

It's not going to get better if you just wait for "time to heal all."

You're not going to overcome depression, heal from trauma, rewire your brain, and become the powerful and resilient guy you're meant to be. I'm saying this to get you to take action for yourself because you deserve it. You've been taught over and over that you don't. The only one that is going to care as much about your happiness and fulfillment in this life is you. It's not a knock on the people in your life—it's just the truth. No one is going to do this work for you. While you're pulling yourself out of this, there are going to be other life hardships that crop up, like break-ups, lost jobs, funerals, and experiences that might cause more trauma that you're going to have to deal with. Life isn't going to come to a halt so that you can heal. This journey is messy—it isn't clean work. There are going to be times when you feel completely lost and isolated. Your depressive mind is going to fight back against what you're doing. When you look at this book sitting on your shelf, your depressive mind might say, "What a sham that was—nothing works."

This is a hard and terrible truth, but it's real. I will always be real with you about the journey.

But, here's the thing. The methodology wasn't built on hopes and dreams. It wasn't built in a vacuum where life's hardships stopped coming at me. It wasn't built by someone that hasn't dealt with debilitating depression. It wasn't built on theory alone. This comes from my real experience of fighting and overcoming depression. It will work, but you have to work too.

The Courage Method is a practical tool that you have to use to overcome depression. Courage is the antithesis to apathy. Build courage to destroy apathy. Stop suppressing pain and surrender to heal pain. Then, get a bunch of people to help you out. No crystals, no chants, no special lights, and no incense. Courage makes it all work. It's the power that's going to get you through this, and if you focus on that, you'll win.

If you follow what I've laid out in this book, get really hungry about going on this journey of self-mastery, and take action, you will emerge victorious.

This is your time my friend—fortune favors the bold.

PART III:

The Journey Begins

"He who jumps into the void owes no explanation to those who stand and watch."
— Jean-Luc Godard

CHAPTER 8:

Releasing from Blame

We've covered a lot of ground in this book so far, but there's one thing that I haven't mentioned that deserves its own chapter: *blame*. It is the one way of being that you need to make a conscious decision to give up. If you don't, it will sabotage your attempt to even get started.

Before we get into this conversation, I want to be very clear that this is not about justifying the perpetrator of your trauma or forcing forgiveness. This is about dissecting and removing a thought construct in your mind that keeps you trapped in a victim mentality, leaving you helpless and unable to take action. Come with me on a mental journey and take this view point, a way to investigate yourself from the outside.

As soon as you blame someone else, you give all of your freedom and power away. You say, "You did this to me! You made me like this! It's your fault that I am the way I am!"

It's true that whatever situation or person that caused your trauma is at fault for what happened to you, but when you continue to blame, you only hurt yourself.

How?

Well, there's a lot more that comes with blame than just a pointed finger. There are payoffs that you get when you blame. You get to be the innocent victim, you get self-pity, and you get to be the recipient of sympathy. I want you to take a look within yourself because when you hear these, you may think, "That doesn't sound like a great payoff." These payoffs satisfy something inside of you. With blame and the payoffs you receive, you ultimately get to be right and justified for being in the position you're in. You get to dodge responsibility. You get to say, "I'm depressed, and everything is so hard because of what happened to me in the past."

With blame in place, you won't be able to be responsible for where you are right now. Responsibility is the ability to access power and be free to take action. When you become responsible for your life, everything starts to change. We often think of responsibility as this heavy-weighted mantle that gets placed on us when entering adulthood, or we think of it as blame, shame, guilt, rightness, or wrongness. That's not it. One of my past therapists noted, "Responsibility is more like respond-ability. The ability to respond." When you live with blame and view yourself as a victim, you have no ability to respond to your current state. This is where the helplessness and hopelessness quality of apathy comes from.

When you were traumatized, you were victimized by someone or something. In that moment, something overpowered your will and did something horrible that you wanted nothing to do with. You have a very good understanding of the impact that has had on your mind and body, but what may be missing is that in that moment or situation, your power to act was stolen from you. Although the trauma has passed, that stolen power, that helplessness, lives on in your mind through blame. It's not what you truly want for yourself. You want the freedom to act, the power to overcome, and to be happy.

Giving up blame grants access to that.

This does not give the person or situation a free pass. This is not forgiveness. This is you being selfish. Give up blame so that you can unhook yourself from trauma and its perpetrator. Once you do that, you can become responsible for everything you are right now, not as blame but access to power and the freedom to take action.

How do you stop blaming?

It's rather simple. Start by asking yourself this question, "How has my blame and feeling like a victim ever helped me?"

You probably won't have any good answers to that question because blame isn't a way to move forward. It's a way of thinking, feeling, and being that keeps you stuck. So, everytime it shows up, you give it up. Look at your life for a moment. Think about times that you've blamed. What has it done for you? Did you blame someone and all of a sudden feel better about what they did to you, or were you stuck with all the bad feelings? Did it add to an internal narrative that said, "Bad things always happen to me."? When you've been blamed, what do you get to be right about? Does this help you classify yourself as the good person, the innocent? Do you enjoy the sympathy you receive from others?

Write a quick list of all the payoffs you receive and all the ways in which you get to be right or good. Then, write a list for all the ways those payoffs keep you from taking action. Finally, write a third list of what life would look like if you stopped blaming—what would you have access to?

Do this and you will deconstruct your victim mentality and unleash your personal power.

CHAPTER 9:

The 4-Phase Battle Plan

In the beginning of this book, I asked you to do one thing. That was to "just read the book." This gives you the time and space to absorb new material and have insights about your experience of depression without being derailed by the depressive mind or being overwhelmed by the battle you have in front of you.

Now that you are nearing the end of this book, you're probably wondering, "How do I implement all of this in my life?"

That's a darn good question! We covered a lot. You've learned how your enemy moves and practical tools and techniques for fighting apathy and healing form trauma. Now, you need a strategy—a methodical way to approach your adversary. You can't just run up the mountain all willy-nilly. You need a battle plan before you go to war.

This is that.

I broke it out into four phases. We'll start with a strong foundation that you can build upon. Like I've said over and over again, this healing path is not linear, and it is also a long-term commitment. I will recommend that each phase take about 60 to 120+ days. The reason for this is because the four phases are built around The Warrior's Way, the habit-building practice for growing your courage muscle. These 60 to 120+ days will help you solidify and layer the 5 core habits.

If you need more time, then you need more time. If you need less time, then you need less time. There's no judgment, no failure, and no weakness in how long or short this takes you. The more you hone the skill of letting yourself go at the pace that you need to go, the closer you will become to knowing yourself and showing care for yourself, which is what we're going for.

Also, keep in mind that this is a structure to keep you focused. If these phases start to get out of order, that's okay. This is your journey of self-discovery. There isn't a "right" way to this, but all of the pieces I've laid out in The Courage Method are an absolute requirement. Remember, you're a car without brakes, and if you install the new braking system without all the pieces, the system will not function properly. You need to build courage, you need healthy habits, you need support, and you need to develop emotional intelligence. With all of that, you will overcome depression.

Let's get started...

Phase One

Tasks to Tackle:

Warrior's Way Habit #1: Make Your Bed

Warrior's Way Habit #2: Keep It Clean

Gather Your Party: Therapist

In phase one, you're going to want to begin by implementing The Warrior's Way into your life. Start with the first two habits that I suggested: making your bed and keeping it clean. We spoke in depth about these in Chapter 7.5, but essentially, it's making a habit of making your bed and keeping your domestic space and personal hygiene tidy and clean. This is going to show yourself that you care about yourself by keeping yourself as clean as possible.

As you start to build those habits, you'll want to get a therapist as soon as possible. You absolutely need that support if you are to win this battle. If you feel resistance to doing this, then this is the perfect opportunity to put that courage muscle to work. In Chapter 11, I will provide a more detailed plan for finding and paying for a therapist. It's going to expedite the process and help you find a therapist in 30 days or less.

Once you've built these two habits (it feels pretty easy to manage them on a daily basis) and you've started therapy, then it's time to move onto phase two.

Phase Two

Tasks to Tackle:

Warrior's Way Habit #3: Freeze Your D*ck Off

Gather Your Party: Trusted Advisor

Practice: Identifying Emotions

In phase two, you need to layer on the third habit from The Warrior's Way: adding regular cold exposure to your routine. I recommend adding 1 to 2 minutes of a cold shower to the end of your daily showers. This is going to help you see that you have some control over your nervous system. You'll hyperventilate at first, but with some practice, you'll be able to slow and deepen your breath, gaining control over your body's response to the cold water. Not only that but it's a refreshing way to wake up your body and mind in the depths of your depression. The next thing that you want to do is start focusing on developing an open and vulnerable relationship with your right-hand man or trusted advisor. Like I mentioned earlier, this might require a bit of courage to open up or start building a new friendship. This is all part of the process—challenging yourself in ways you never have before. If you can master that, then you can achieve anything you want.

Now, with your therapist, you are probably going to start digging into your past and some of the painful emotions that you're experiencing. This is a great time to start to explore those emotions and your triggers. In the Art of Alchemy, we discussed a method for identifying and tracking your feelings on a day-to-day basis. You can either use the feeling wheel found in this book or from another resource, or you can use one of the apps that I suggest in the resource section. By learning to pause and identify your emotions, you will be on your way to being able to regulate your emotions and triggers.

While you do this work, it's an excellent time to also start to observe your emotional and physiological experiences. What are the moments, situations, senses, or people that pull your trigger? What are the emotions and feelings that come up? What does it look like after you've been triggered? Do you go into deeper depressive episodes? Do your self-punishing thoughts intensify?

You can of course start to use The Letting Go Technique to manage your triggers and deeper depressive episodes, but don't feel like you need to have mastery over it. You can focus on that more in phase three. Right now, it's all about noticing, identifying, and tracking your triggers and the emotional states they put you in. Then, you'll start to see more clearly what or who it is in your life that caused you trauma and better understand how it influences you now. Instead of being frustrated with yourself or punishing yourself, acknowledge that the things that happened to you were not your fault and that it's time to start showing yourself a little bit more love as you process this pain.

Phase Three

Tasks to Tackle:

Warrior's Way Habit #4: Move Your Body

Gather Your Party: Trainer

Practice: Emotional Regulation

At this point in the battle with depression, you've established some great habits and are starting to get a better understanding of your past and how it influences your present. Not only that but you've started to build a fantastic support system to help you overcome this depression. At this point, you're going to want to start to explore what type of physical exercise you want to build as a habit in your life. It might take some time, especially if you're not the type of person that naturally gravitates towards exercise. In the process of figuring out what kind of physical exercise you want to do, you can also add another party member to your crew: the trainer! We explored this in depth in Chapter 7.7. Feel free to go back if you need some support or ideas for finding the perfect trainer.

I wouldn't be surprised if this takes a little bit longer than the others because building an exercise habit is not easy. This is going to be an amazing way to build your courage muscle because of the challenge it presents. At this point, you've already strengthened your courage muscle in building smaller habits. It might take a little extra push, but I know you can do it. Once you build this exercise habit, you're going to intensify your courage building because every time you work out, especially if you have a trainer, they are going to push you through discomfort, thereby building more courage.

At this point, you've also identified a lot of your triggers and you understand where they lead you in your mind and in your heart.

Now, you can start putting The Letting Go Technique to use to regulate those triggering experiences. The regular practice of doing this technique will start to rewire how you think and how you feel in those instances. It's a tremendous opportunity to turn off your automatic emotion suppression system and start letting go and healing from the pain you've been holding onto. Remember, depression is suppressed pain. When you stop suppressing pain and deal with it head on, you start to clear up apathy and self-punishing thoughts. Then, something else emerges: self-esteem, confidence, and excitement about life.

Phase Four

Tasks to Tackle:

Warrior's Way Habit #5: Eat Well

Gather Your Party: Backups

Once you've made it to the fourth phase of the battle plan, you will have built a tremendous amount of courage. You're dealing with your pain head on and you're starting to see the benefits of The Courage Method. You're able to identify and regulate your emotions, you've built regular habits to show yourself that you care about yourself, and you have people around you to support you.

During this fourth phase, you're going to start adding a healthy eating habit. This calls for some exploration on your part of what is going to work best for you. Like I mentioned in Chapter 7.5, I tried multiple different diets to find what worked best for me. All of them were beneficial to my journey and helped me get a better understanding of myself and what my body requires. In this journey, I was also able to learn a lot about how the body works and how to nourish it for depression. I urge you to go on this journey and reclaim power over your own health and physiology. The main idea here is that you build a healthy diet that is based on whole foods.

Next, you will want to start to gather your backups. These are friends, family, and community members that you feel that you can be vulnerable and honest with. These are the people that will support you in the hardest times during this battle with depression. Also, during this fourth phase, you're going to want to reflect on all the work that you've done so far. What you have done is a tremendous task and is no small feat.

Keep Calm and Fight On

After you have implemented all four phases of the battle plan, it doesn't mean that your work is complete. It means you have transcended the teacher, and it is time to take this journey to a more personal level. You've built the required structures you need to be able to identify and regulate emotions, process your trauma, and live a full life. At this point, you've built a system in your life that will continue to support you in your mental and emotional health.

All of your triggers may not have disappeared, and you still may experience depressive episodes, general feelings of apathy, and even self-punishing thoughts. It only means that you need to continue fighting the battle. There will be times where you feel as though it's all cleared before a bad trigger brings you back to some of your worst feelings. You keep fighting and you keep letting go and healing. The only way out is through, and with courage, you will get through. It doesn't just take time to heal. It takes consistent and continued effort. The more work that you put into understanding yourself and your condition, the more often you will be able to release pain.

But really, this is the good part.

This is the part where you get such a depth of understanding of yourself that you're able to draw boundaries with toxic people and are able to choose the right friends and partners in your life. You can start to chase after "your purpose," which we'll identify in the next chapter. The deeper you go into the dark spaces of your psyche and of your past, the more you will know yourself. With that, life opens up for you, and you'll achieve any of the mental, emotional, and life goals you can dream up.

CHAPTER 10:

Clear the Slate

To deploy The Courage Method in your life you need to get focused. It's time to clear the slate of everything that happened in the past so that you can move on with your life. One of the modern problems that we must deal with is distraction. Not only are we distracted by our phones every day but we are distracted by all the things we're told we need to do and all the things we need to become to feel fulfilled. This is an absolute distraction to overcoming depression.

We are very good at not dealing with what is directly in front of us. It's not that we're not good at it, but we're taught to ignore it because why would you want to focus on the things that hurt? We're taught to look for the positive and to gravitate towards feeling good through external accomplishment and validation.

If we continue to avoid and resist the pain that is directly in front of us, we're only going to prolong our suffering. Those external accomplishments and validations are never going to make that pain go away. You can spend the rest of your life searching for external happiness and feel depressed for the entirety of your life. In fact, it's so easy to do if you want to make the rest of your life miserable—just ignore your pain. That's all you have to do. Let your mind distract you and think about other things. Work towards all of your external goals and ignore your internal world.

If you want to truly heal, focus on what's directly in front of you. Don't worry about all the things that you're going to do in the future, how you're going to do them, and whether or not you're going to fail. Focus on what's directly in front of you. That's your depression and your trauma. When you do that, you can clear the slate and pain from your internal world.

Then, you become a different person. The thoughts that you have about yourself change, the ways that you feel about yourself change, and who you are at your core shifts. All of the self-punishing thoughts, the apathy and the horrible things you've endured, are no longer there to tell you who you are. Once that's cleared, you get to decide who you want to be in the world. You make decisions for yourself based on a positive self-image and a clear mind. Then, you have all of the healthy habits you've built and energy to throw at whatever you want in your life. This is what happens when you clear the slate. The way that I learned to do this over the last decade was by *redefining purpose*. As men, we search for some kind of purpose in life, something to work towards and fulfill our need to contribute to the community, people, and the world.

There's this whole conversation about your purpose and what you're meant for. To me, it's just that there are things that you do and there are things that you don't do in your life. There are different times when you do things and different times when you don't do things. I think this whole idea of purpose and your true meaning in life confuses us more than it helps. If you're always on this kind of search of what you're truly meant for, then you're going to project that all over your life. You'll be in a constant search for purpose and ignoring what's in front of you right now.

This idea of purpose sounds like it's been manufactured to have us chasing after something, right? Is your true purpose the thing that's going to make you a million dollars? Is the meaning of your true purpose something that you're really, really good at?

I don't know.

There are some people that spend their whole lives playing piano and they're really talented at that. Is that their one true purpose in life? Maybe it's part of it, but maybe at different times in their lives, their purpose is taking care of kids. I'm dancing around the idea and playing with this strange idea of purpose. To me, purpose can be more practical and less dreamy or confusing. Your purpose is what's in front of you. Anything else is a distraction.

Especially when you're dealing with depression.

You need something to do with all of those external desires and things that you want to accomplish. We need to be able to leverage them to draw you into the future but not distract you from waging total war on depression. I want you to draw a pyramid on a piece of paper with four sections top to bottom. The first step is to identify where you want to go and don't confuse it too much or ask too many questions. Go based on your initial desires. Where do you want to be? Is it that you want to be living off the grid, working remotely, and have a family? Do you want to live the city life with a high-rise Manhattan apartment, working on broadway stages?

Don't think about it too much. Gut reactions. Think about the things that you think about a lot in life and think, "Oh man, I wish my life was like that!"

Write that little dream at the top of the pyramid.

The second step is understanding how you're going to get there. What are the five things you need to get there? These are five things that you may need to do over the next 3 to 5 years. For the off-the-grid example, it might look like this:

1. Find an industry that has remote jobs.

2. Get training and experience in that industry.

3. Get hired in that industry.

4. Find out how to finance land.

5. Learn about how to live off the grid (solar, farming, water collection, etc.).

Write your five things in the next section of the pyramid beneath the top.

For the next step, I want you to think about trying to do all of those steps while you're in the mental and emotional state that you're in now. Seriously think about it on a day-to-day basis. Does it look hard? Does it seem almost impossible? Does it feel overwhelming?

Now we're getting to the good stuff. Would it not be wise to make overcoming depression your main focus BEFORE you go after that big, external goal?

I'm sure that the answer is yes, so in the third section, write "Overcome Depression." In the bottom spot of that pyramid, you can just go ahead and write "The Courage Method." I know the exercise is rigged, but the purpose is to get you to see that focusing on your internal world first is going to help you get where you want to go. It's not the glorious and validating work you might want to do, but it's the best way to approach it... if you want to be happy. That big, external desire gives you something to motivate you through the process of overcoming depression. It's something to look forward to and be excited about. Right now, I just want you to make a commitment to yourself to let your internal world be your purpose. It's what's directly in front of you, and this is your time to clear the slate.

CHAPTER 11:

How to Find a Therapist in 30 days

When I was in some of the worst years of my depression, I knew I needed a therapist. I had one previously when I was at college, but it was not that simple anymore. I didn't have insurance through my employer, and I didn't have the money to pay $100 or more a week for therapy. For a long time, I complained about it and avoided taking any action. It was towards the end of the year, and my HR department asked if I wanted insurance through them or if I wanted to get insurance through the state. It was the first time that I had even thought about or looked into it. I was in my late 20s and started to think that I ought to start doing adult-type things. There was a deadline too. I had to figure out what I was going to do or I'd go another year without insurance and without therapy. That courage muscle was activated, and I committed myself to learning everything I could about this whole insurance thing. I'll spare you the details I experienced of searching for insurance terms on Google, calling my mother, and getting pissed at what a sham it all is.

But, I decided that the insurance plan through the state would be the most beneficial because it was actually going to cover all mental health services. After filling out a stack of online government forms, within a few weeks, I was sent my insurance card. Now, I had another obstacle: finding a therapist. I tried a myriad different ways, from googling "therapist near me" to searching for "therapist" on Google maps and clicking on different practices and trying to call them. This process was tedious, and it was touch-and-go for months without any results.

Then, after a particularly severe trigger and being stuck in bed for an entire weekend, I got pissed off again. I was so mad about how complicated it was, how many therapists didn't have room on their calendars, and that I had to get it done while dealing with crippling depression. The anger led to discovering the fastest and easiest way to find a therapist. I discovered psychologytoday.com and learned that you could search by area, filter by whether or not they were accepting new patients, modality, insurance, gender, and so much more. Not only that but you could message the therapists directly on the platform.

During this time, I had been also been working as a freelance copywriter and marketer. With freelancing, a massive part of your job is getting new clients, and when you're new, no one knows you. You have to do a LOT of cold outreach via LinkedIn or email. When you do cold outreach, everything is about the numbers. If you reach out to 100 people a week and 20 people respond, you have a 20% response rate. Of those 20 people, 4 people might get on a call with you. If you have 1 of those people book your services, then you have a whopping 1% conversion rate, which is pretty good... That's 4 clients a month. The thing about cold outreach is that you don't craft a new message each time—you use a template. Once you've got a list of people, it's all copy, paste, and send.

I applied this same idea to getting a therapist.

Instead of getting precious about finding the 'perfect therapist for me,' crafting the right message to them, or worrying about what they'd think of me, I treated it like a numbers game. So, I wrote a quick, 75-word template, jumped on psychologytoday.com, searched my area, and filtered by accepting new patients, male therapists, takes BCBS insurance, and remote only. There sat a list of 25+ therapists that could be my potential, new therapist, and I went to town. I messaged 20 therapists in under 8 minutes, and within the week, I had set up 3 consultations. Within a week, after those consults, I worked with a therapist whom I stayed with for almost two years. I probably would have stayed longer had I not moved out of state. At the end of this chapter, I will provide you with the templates I use whenever I'm in the market for a therapist.

This path is not just about fighting your inner demons, understanding trauma, and healing from pain. There are external obstacles where you have to leverage courage to overcome them. One of them is figuring out how to pay for therapy and fighting for the care you deserve. It's a pain, it's confusing, there are forms involved, and whenever you have to do this, you're guaranteed to get annoyed. This is why we practice courage—so that you can take action when there's resistance and get the results you want.

If you don't have insurance and your employer doesn't offer plans, your first step is going to be going to healthcare.gov to see if you qualify for Medicaid or a marketplace plan. I've known people who qualified for Medicaid and had their mental health services completely covered. I've used the marketplace plans and either paid $50-$75 a month or had my mental health services completely covered. If you spend 15-20 minutes on a few websites filling out some boxes with your information, you might be eligible for some pretty good insurance.

This is how it works as of 2024. Go to healthcare.gov and fill out the first form to see if you're eligible for either Medicaid or a marketplace plan. If you are eligible for Medicaid, then you can begin the Medicaid application. If you're not eligible for Medicaid, you will be taken to a new form to see if you're eligible for a marketplace plan, and most people are. The marketplace plans are insurance plans that the government subsidizes, which means they pay part of the monthly premium (payment). Instead of paying $600+ a month, you'll pay as low as $0/month. Depending on your income, they will pay more or less of the monthly premium. When you complete the second form, you will be able to start your application on healthcare.gov or you will be redirected to your state marketplace site to start your application since not all states use healthcare.gov.

Once you've completed the application, there may be a wait time while you get an approved set of insurance plans that you can choose from. Once you get this approved set of plans, then you have a decision to make. Choose a plan that's affordable and gets you mental health coverage. You can reach out to marketplace support and inquire about which plans will get you mental health coverage. I highly recommend that you spend some time looking up the different types of plans and all the insurance lingo they use. It will take some time to learn, but again, this is part of the journey. Honestly, we should have a better healthcare system. We should be taught all of this in high school, but this is where we are. You're going to have to do everything it takes to get the care you deserve so that you can break free from this depression.

If you can't get insurance, your plan doesn't cover it, or you have an extremely high deductible, then your other option is to pay out of pocket. Almost every therapist offers a sliding scale payment option. This means that they will accept a lower per-session rate than their normal rate. Sometimes, there's a limit to how low they will go, but I've seen some therapists go as low as $50 a session. You have to ask if you need it. Use your courage to overcome any thoughts or fears about your worth attached to the financial support you may need right now. They created these sliding scales to give people more access to care. They've built their practices so that when some people pay top dollar and other people pay within their sliding scale range, they arrive at their goal in terms of revenue. Don't worry about them—take care of yourself. In the outreach templates below, I've included one for those with insurance and another for those without insurance inquiring about sliding scale.

I made this as simple as possible for you so that you can focus on building that courage up within yourself. Start clicking buttons, setting filters, filling out forms, and getting the care you need to overcome this depression.

Getting a therapist is almost as important as building courage in this journey. So, fight for it—fight for yourself. If you have to tighten your budget to pay for it—do it. If you can only afford one session a month—do it. If you need to ask for financial support from friends or family—do it. Whatever you do, don't pass on getting a therapist. It's not going to be like this forever, and going to therapy is going to help relieve the pressure of the pain you're holding inside and help you tell the stories you need to tell. After some time, things are going to open up, and when you're healing, you'll start to step into a new future that you can't possibly imagine today.

Just keep going.

Outreach Templates

Below are two templates that you can copy word for word. Once you've got a list of therapists from psychologytoday.com, then you can customize this template to send to as many of those therapists as you want. The more you send, the better!

Outreach Template with Insurance

Hi there,

My name is [YOUR NAME]. I am looking for a therapist that can help me with depression. I currently have insurance through [INSURANCE COMPANY NAME]. Do you take that insurance?

Also, can you tell me more about how you work with clients who have depression? If we both think this is a good match, can we set up a short, 15-20 minute consultation to see if we'd be a good fit?

Thanks so much,

[NAME]

Outreach Template without Insurance

Hi there,

My name is [YOUR NAME]. I'm looking for a therapist that can help me with depression. I currently do not have insurance. Do you offer a sliding scale for payment?

Also, can you tell me more about how you work with clients who have depression? If we both think this is a good match, can we set up a short 15-20 minute consultation to see if we'd be a good fit? Thanks so much,

[YOUR NAME]

CHAPTER 12:

Conclusion

I hope that while reading this book you've had life-changing insights and have a better understanding of depression and how to overcome it.

Let's recap what we've covered:

- In the first few chapters, we dug into what your life looks like now and what it can look like after overcoming depression.

- We explored the problems that you're facing with a few assessments and started to prescribe a few solutions. It started to become clear how The Courage Method could help you heal from your trauma and overcome depression.

- In the next few chapters, we got very real about what this journey is going to take with the **5 Hard and Ugly Truths about Depression**.

- Then, we revealed the powerhouse that's going to help you get through this perilous journey—that's courage. You learned that courage isn't just a word but a psychological phenomenon that you have the ability to grow just like a muscle.

- In Part II of this book, we explained everything you need to heal from your trauma and overcome depression with **The 3 Arts of Self-Mastery**.

- You gained a deeper understanding of the inner workings of depression and trauma which led to a series of solutions, including The **Warrior's Way**, a habit-building method to develop your courage muscle, and **The Letting Go Technique**, a simple, 4-step process for regulating emotions and triggers.

- Then, we focused on gathering your party who are the rag-tag, loyal people in your life that are going to help you on this journey. You know now that you can't go it alone, and you know who to call on.

- Finally, we finished the book with the **4-Phase Battle Plan** and made this journey your main priority so that you can clear the slate of your life.

In the beginning of this book, I made the recommendation to, "Just read the book," without distraction or worry about how to implement the method.

The next step is simple.

Take new action.

You don't have to worry about doing it perfectly. Just take action on this method. Get started. Don't file this away in your mind and carry on with what you've been doing.

Remember, courage is the feeling, "There is a storm coming. I'm going to meet it and overcome it at all odds." Focus yourself on building your courage muscle so that it can drive you forward in the hardest parts of this journey. It is the power behind the rest of the method, and it is the antithesis of apathy.

If you develop courage, face your pain head on, and surround yourself with an epic party—you will vanquish depression.

In the beginning of this book, I asked you to send an email letting me know that you were undertaking the journey. If you haven't, you have that opportunity again by emailing me directly at dylan@dylanmartinsen.com. You can also use the QR code below to sign up for updates on upcoming books to help you become the man you're meant to be.

https://bit.ly/djmlist

Fight like hell, my friend.

Dylan Martinsen

Resources

Suicide Hotline: If you or someone you know is experiencing suicidal thoughts or a crisis, please reach out immediately to the Suicide Prevention Lifeline at 800-273-8255 or text HOME to the Crisis Text Line at 741741. These services are free and confidential.

Recommended Reads:

The Iceman: Wim Hof by Wim Hof

Letting Go: The Pathway of Surrender by David R. Hawkins

Breathe: The New Science of a Lost Art by James Nestor

Grit: The Power of Passion and Perseverance by Angela Duckworth

Apps:

How We Feel
Identifying and Tracking Emotions
www.howwefeel.org

Daylio
Mood Tracker
www.daylio.net

Types of Therapy:

1. Cognitive Behavioral Therapy (CBT): A widely used form of therapy that focuses on identifying and changing negative thought patterns and behaviors. It helps individuals develop coping strategies and problem-solving skills to manage their mental health issues.

2. Acceptance and Commitment Therapy (ACT): Encourages individuals to accept their thoughts and feelings rather than fight them. It emphasizes living in accordance with one's values and taking committed actions toward personal goals.

3. Dialectical Behavior Therapy (DBT): A type of CBT that emphasizes the balance between acceptance and change. It teaches skills in mindfulness, distress tolerance, emotional regulation, and interpersonal effectiveness.

Particularly useful for individuals with borderline personality disorder.

4. Psychodynamic Therapy: This approach explores how unconscious thoughts and past experiences influence current behavior and emotions. It aims to increase self-awareness and understanding of the influence of the past on present behavior.

5. Humanistic Therapy: Focuses on the individual's capacity for self-awareness and personal growth. Techniques such as client-centered therapy (developed by Carl Rogers) emphasize a non-judgmental, empathetic, therapeutic environment.

6. Eye Movement Desensitization and Reprocessing (EMDR): A specialized therapy for trauma and PTSD that uses guided eye movements to help individuals process and integrate traumatic memories.

7. Interpersonal Therapy (IPT): Focuses on improving interpersonal relationships and social functioning to help reduce distress. It addresses issues such as grief, role transitions, and conflicts with others.

8. Somatic Therapy: Integrates the mind and body, recognizing the role of the body in storing trauma and emotional distress. Techniques include bodily awareness,

breathing exercises, and physical movement to release tension and trauma.

9. Narrative Therapy: Centers on the stories people tell about their lives. It helps individuals reframe their experiences and create empowering narratives, recognizing their strengths and abilities to overcome challenges.

Works Cited:

Studies

Colcombe, Stanley J., et al. "Aerobic Exercise Training Increases Brain Volume in Aging Humans." *The Journals of Gerontology: Series A* 61, no. 11 (2006): 1166-1170. https://doi.org/10.1093/gerona/61.11.1166.

Harfmann, Brian D., et al. "Acute Cold Exposure and Its Effect on Catecholamine Release in Humans." *Journal of Applied Physiology* 98, no. 1 (2005): 162-169. https://doi.org/10.1152/japplphysiol.01007.2004.

Lang, Peter J., Margaret M. Bradley, and Bruce N. Cuthbert. "Emotion, Motivation, and Anxiety: Brain Mechanisms and Psychophysiology." *Biological Psychiatry* 44, no. 12 (1998): 1248-1263. https://www.ncbi.nlm.nih.gov/pmc/articles/PMC3505409/#:~:text=Therefore%2C%20it%20may%20be%20 helpful,motivation%20until%20the%20habit%20 forms.

Moncrieff, Joanna. "The Chemical Imbalance Theory of Depression: Still Promoted but Still Unfounded." Joanna Moncrieff (blog). May 1, 2014. https://joannamoncrieff.com/2014/05/01/the-chemical-imbalance-theory-of-depression-still-promoted-but-still-unfounded/.

Moncrieff, Joanna, Ruth E. Cooper, Tom Stockmann, Simone Amendola, Michael Pascal Hengartner, and Mark A. Horowitz. "The Serotonin Theory of Depression: A Systematic Umbrella Review of the Evidence." *Molecular Psychiatry* 28, no. 8 (2022): 3243-3256. https://doi.org/10.1038/s41380-022-01661-0.

Ozbay, Fatih, Douglas C. Johnson, Eleni Dimoulas, Caroline Morgan, Dennis Charney, and Steven Southwick. "Social Support and Resilience to Stress: From Neurobiology to Clinical Practice." *Psychiatry (Edgmont)* 4, no. 5 (2007): 35-40. https://www.ncbi.nlm.nih.gov/pmc/articles/PMC2921311/.

Parvizi, Josef, and Vinod Menon. "The Will to Persevere Induced by Electrical Stimulation of the Human Cingulate Gyrus." *Neuron* 80, no. 6 (2013): 1359-1367. https://doi.org/10.1016/j.neuron.2013.09.057.

Parvizi, Josef, and David L. Strangman. "The Tenacious Brain: How the Anterior Mid-Cingulate Contributes to Achieving Goals." *Cortex* 47, no. 8 (2011): 1100-1111. https://doi.org/10.1016/j.cortex.2011.05.013.

Srámek, P., M. Simecková, L. Janský, J. Savlíková, and S. Vybíral. "Human Physiological Responses to Immersion into Water of Different Temperatures." *European Journal of Applied Physiology* 81, no. 5 (2000): 436-42. https://doi.org/10.1007/s004210050065.

Walsh, Froma. "The Role of Social Support in Resilience: Examining Its Role in Families, Communities, and Organizations." *Psychiatry* 70, no. 3 (2007): 175-198. https://doi.org/10.1521/psyc.2007.70.3.175.

Books

Duckworth, Angela. *Grit: The Power of Passion and Perseverance*. New York: Scribner, 2016.

Hawkins, David R. *Letting Go: The Pathway of Surrender*. Sedona, AZ: Veritas Publishing, 2012.

Hayes, Steven C., Kirk D. Strosahl, and Kelly G. Wilson. *Acceptance and Commitment Therapy: An Experiential Approach to Behavior Change*. New York: Guilford Press, 1999.

Hof, Wim. *The Ice Man: Wim Hof.* Amsterdam: Inside Out Publishing, 2011.

Levine, Peter A. *Waking the Tiger: Healing Trauma.* Berkeley, CA: North Atlantic Books, 1997.

Ogden, Pat, Kekuni Minton, and Clare Pain. *Trauma and the Body: A Sensorimotor Approach to Psychotherapy.* New York: W. W. Norton & Company, 2006.

Van der Kolk, Bessel A. *The Body Keeps the Score: Brain, Mind, and Body in the Healing of Trauma.* New York: Penguin Books, 2014.

Walker, Brian Browne. *The I Ching or Book of Changes: A Guide to Life's Turning Points.* New York: St. Martin's Press, 1992.

About the Author

Dylan Martinsen has dedicated his life to helping people through various outlets throughout his life, including martial arts, massage therapy, theater, and writing. He craves mastery in what he loves most: martial arts and writing. Yet, his highest goal is to make life easier and more joyful for the men who cross his path.

For over two decades, Dylan has been on the hunt for understanding not only what it means to be a "good man" but to live a fulfilled and purposeful life. Through his own traumas and challenges, he's identified the modern man's obstacles on the journey for authentic happiness. He uses his talents in writing and speaking to make an impact not just for men but the lives of the people around them.

When he's not writing, Dylan loves training in Ving Tsun Kung Fu, exploring the Blue Ridge Mountains of Western North Carolina, and spending time with his partner, Ben, and three dogs, Oak, Bear, and Mopsy.

Dylan believes in the power of the person. Anyone can overcome their circumstances as long as they are willing to look within and transform themselves. The journey is perilous, but with the help of some friends, continued effort, and mental flexibility—it's the grandest and bravest adventure anyone could embark on.

All inquiries for podcast appearances, video shows, and speaking can be sent to dylan@dylanmartinsen.com

Made in United States
North Haven, CT
19 August 2024